A YEAR IN CORNWALL

WITH

TIM HUBBARD

Illustrated by Sue Lewington

TRURAN

First published in 2000 by Truran, Croft Prince, Mount Hawke, Truro,
Cornwall TR4 8EE

ISBN 1 85022 147 2

Printed and bound in Cornwall by R. Booth (Bookbinder) Ltd & Troutbeck Press,
Antron Hill, Mabe, Penryn, Cornwall TR10 9HH

Main text set in Novarese

Quotation from For the Fallen by Laurence Binyon on page 77 by kind permission
of the Society of Authors, on behalf of the Laurence Binyon Estate.

The quotation on page 12 is from God's Garden by Dorothy Frances Gurney.

Front Cover photograph: Padstow May Day - Simon Burt
Back Cover photograph: Tim at BBC Radio Cornwall - Simon Burt

THE YEAR

A Winter's Sunday Afternoon Walk
Down the Garden Path...
Flying the Flag on St Piran's Day
The Western Hunt Point to Point
A Dawn Chorus at Heligan
Spending a Weekend on Scilly
May Day in Padstow
Helston Flora Day
The Royal Cornwall Show
Point and Penpoll Regatta
A Summer's Day on the Beach
Gwennap Village Fete
Falmouth Classics Week
Sitting in the sun at Minions
The Newlyn Fish Festival
Walking "Coast to Coast"
Surfers Against Sewage Ball
Lantern-Making Workshop
A Woodland Day at Trelissick Garden
Truro's City of Lights
The Mousehole Lights

For my parents, Mark and Pat Hubbard, both of whom knew Cornwall as children and who, years later, have discovered it all over again.

FOREWORD

When I first came to Cornwall well over twenty years ago I had no idea that it would become my home. Now the county's become the focus of both my professional and my private life and so when I was offered the chance to write about my *Year in Cornwall* it seemed like a good way of celebrating the place in which I live and work.

Over the past twelve months I've been to just some of the hundreds of public events which take place each year from Land's End to the Tamar. The one thing they share, I think, is that they all reflect a very Cornish view of the world in one of the increasingly few parts of the UK where a sense of community and "pride of place" is still strong. Many of them, like May Day in Padstow and Flora Day in Helston, are annual events so traditional that it seems as though life in those towns revolves around them entirely. Others - such as the regattas and the horse races - are family fun days out and then there are those relatively new festivals such as City of Lights which are gradually establishing themselves as important dates on the Cornish calendar.

Alongside the public events I also wanted to write about the personal days out that many of us are able to enjoy each year. You can make the most of the Cornish countryside or coast - a winter walk or a summer's day on the beach - at any time of the year or, of course, you can stay at home pottering around the garden and enjoy your own bit of the landscape.

Living in Cornwall makes you a member of a very special club although everyone has their own reasons why it's so important to them. You'll find some of mine in my *Year in Cornwall*.

ACKNOWLEDGEMENTS

Thanks are due to Ivan and Heather Corbett who originally approached me with the idea of writing, rather than speaking, for a change. At the BBC, Pauline Causey and Leo Devine gave their support to the project and I'd also like to thank - apart from those people I've been able to mention personally - everyone I met at the dozens of events I went to during the year and who shared the stories and secrets of their own years in Cornwall to help make mine so special.

More than anything else, I'd like to pay tribute to Sue Lewington for drawing what I saw with such wit and perception and, beyond the pages, to Pete Thomas, of course, for everything else.

A WINTER'S SUNDAY AFTERNOON WALK
January

Like hitting your head against a brick wall, you know it'll feel good when you stop, but a walk on a Sunday afternoon in the winter isn't always the first thing to spring to mind. There you are, full and sleepy after a Sunday lunch with the family and just looking forward to an afternoon dozing in front of the fire with the Sunday supplements and an old black and white film on the telly, when someone has to say it.

"Does anyone want to go for a walk?"

Everyone surreptitiously looks at each other under their eyelids hoping that the question won't be picked up and that somebody will change the subject quickly. Too late.

"Yes, what a lovely idea; the rain'll probably hold off 'til later."

The die is cast. There's no backing out now. Not wanting to seem lazy/unfit/unwilling to join in the so-called "fun" or, worse, be accused of spoiling A Family Event ("Why don't we do things all together any more?") you force a smile and, with it, yourself out of your chair.

Next comes the big debate of where to go.

"Perranporth beach?"

"The tide's too far in."

"Vault beach?"

"The tide's too far out."

"Bodmin Moor?"

"Too far to drive."

"Zennor cliffs?"

"Too windy."

It's at this point that you think that you may be in for a reprieve. You take a stand.

"And it is going to rain. Shall we, er, just stay here?"

No response so you bring out the big guns and add

"We could sort out the holiday photographs..."

A pause. It's something that you've been asked to do, nagged about even, on and off, for the past year but now your words fall on stony ground.
"No, let's just go and see where we end up."

Of all the most ridiculous comments whenever you're deciding where to go this one takes the biscuit. Yes, I know that in books and films people set out for a drive or a walk or whatever and apparently just come across the perfect pub, the most beautiful beach or the prettiest village but, let's face it, you're far more likely to end up in a field in the middle of nowhere or in an empty rain lashed town on early closing day. For now, though, there's no turning back. Three adults, two children and a dog begin The Big Adventure. Coats and jackets and scarves, gloves and hats and umbrellas are piled together in the hall. The dog's lead (the training sessions never worked), an old towel (muddy paws) and a packet of mints (bribes for those rabbit temptation moments) are heaped on top.
"Are we ready?"
"Well, I'll just..."
"In a minute when..."
"Can I just watch the end of 'East Enders'?"

Having eventually mustered the troops and squeezed everyone in, it only takes about five minutes for every car window to be running with condensation as our collective breaths do battle with the car's heater and then only another five for the children to start arguing.
"If you two aren't going to behave we'll have to go home..." comes the threat and I have to restrain myself. If I joined in could I go home too? Please?

Pulling out of the lane onto the main road the first heavy drops of rain thwack on to the windscreen. You often hear on the radio or read in the newspaper that Cornwall lacks wet-weather attractions for its visitors, but it's only on days like these that you realise how true it is and what the poor souls looking for something to do in the dry actually have to put up with. Short of joining the hundreds of people mooching around one of the DIY superstores or lurking around in the indoor parts of garden centres, a wet January afternoon didn't offer many alternatives.

 By the tried and tested formula of taking the first right turn, then the second left, first right, second left, over and over again we "seemed to end up" in Newquay. Driving into the town the road was lined with semi-detached guesthouses "The Palms", "Sunsets" and even "Bacardi". Anyone would have thought we were in the Caribbean but the fact that the swinging house signs were held parallel to the ground by the wind and their net curtained windows were streaming

with rain somehow gave the game away. Inside lights glowed and TV sets flickered. "No vacancies" signs might as well have read "You must be mad to think we'd even open the front door" and plastic dustbin lids blew around like tumbleweed in a Western.

There's nothing sadder than a seaside town out of season and on this particular January day Newquay looked pretty sad, let me tell you. "Open in the Spring" was one of the more hopeful signs left on shop doorways. Most just said "Closed", "Shut for the Winter" or, more ominously, "We won't be back for some time". Amusement arcades lay idle and gaudy fluorescent signs advertising surfboard hire or cheap beer looked very much the worse for wear.

Of course in the summer the story's very different. Some years back the town sold itself as a cheap and cheerful beach resort and the plethora of pubs, clubs and discos meant that it attracted crowds and crowds of young people whose behaviour didn't always go down well with the locals. Nowadays, despite surf and

rock music festivals and the 'Run to the Sun' car rally where the object of the exercise seems to soak everyone taking part with as much water (and other more doubtful substances) as possible, the emphasis seems to be on attracting families in the summer and older people out of season. For the visitor, the area around the harbour is still full of interest, there's the old huer's hut and the island with its curious house perched on the top and of course the beaches are some of the most impressive in Europe.

Newquay's a curious place, I always think, because despite the theme pubs and the tacky souvenir shops there's still a real town lurking underneath. For the people who live there it's still a town where you can shop, go to the doctor or the dentist, send your children to school and carry on a relatively normal life although you can never quite forget that it's a place which, by and large, survives on the money it can make in three months of the year. I remember waiting in the bank in Newquay's main street one day, while in front of me in the queue was a woman chatting away to her friend, a personal stereo plugged into the other ear, drinking a can of coke and with nothing on but a bikini!

No visitors to be seen today, though, just a couple of people with anorak hoods pulled tightly around their faces leaning into the wind and dragging reluctant dogs behind them. With nowhere to get even a cup of tea in sight, we drove on and met up with the beaches again at Porth. The stretch of coastline from Newquay up to Padstow is an odd mix of the "bungaloid" development so criticised by the late poet laureate and great fan of Cornwall Sir John Betjeman, wonderful cliffs and beaches, rolling countryside and some impressive old stone-built farms and country houses. The road dips up and down as you head north from beach level, where the sand blows over the road, to cliff top height where you can see for miles up and down the coast.

By this point in the afternoon we were getting desperate to get the children and ourselves - let alone the dog - out of the car and so we pulled in at Watergate Bay. Now if I was in charge of traffic arrangements for Cornwall I think I'd forget all about "Park and Ride" schemes (where you pay over the odds to park your car in a field miles out of the town you want to visit and then wait for a bus which sometimes never comes) and start up "Park and Read" schemes. The idea's very simple and from what we saw that Sunday afternoon, and on lots of afternoons after that, it'd be a huge hit. As we pulled up I realised that we were not alone - a long line of cars, windows steamed up, were parked facing the sea. In every single one families and couples were sitting - some with flasks and sandwiches - reading the Sunday papers and quietly dozing. Occasionally hands would appear on the windscreens wiping a clear patch through which anxious faces would peer and then subside back into the fug.

Since then I've seen "Park and Read"-ers everywhere - Falmouth's Pendennis Head is a good place to spot them, Long Rock car park looking over to St Michael's Mount is another. Now we joined them ourselves and, as the rain seemed to have let up for a moment, spilled out of the car and on to the beach. For a few minutes we forgot it was mid-winter. After an hour or so cooped up together it was a chance for everyone to let off steam. The dog tried to lap up the contents of every rock pool he could find, the children played an energetic game of I'll-try-to-push-you-in-the-sea-before-you-can-push-me and we took deep breaths and struggled, hands stuffed deep into coat pockets, against the force of the wind.

Ten minutes later we were back in the car and were heading home but we were a very different group from the one that had arrived. Red cheeks and hair plastered to our faces, our eyes sparkled and even the dog shaking wet sand all over us couldn't stop the grins. As we arrived back home the curtains had not been drawn in the house next door. Looking through the windows I could see their family sprawled around the living room hypnotised by the glowing box in the corner.

That I felt smug was an understatement because, of course, it was really me who'd wanted to go out all along...

DOWN THE GARDEN PATH...
February

Aren't gardeners a lovely lot? They are, you know. Try to think of a gardener you don't like and I'll bet you'll be struggling. People tell me it's because people who garden are either "in touch with their roots" (sorry!) or are "down to earth" (sorry again!!) and that of course they're

Nearer God's heart in a garden
Than anywhere else on earth.

Now before I go any further I want to say that when I talk about gardeners I mean someone who actually knows a thing or two about plants and how to grow them, and who enjoys the (endless and pretty hard) work of making a bit of land their very own bit of heaven. To my mind they're a very different breed to the sort of person who tips ten tons of pink gravel all over their soil, puts in a bit of blue decking and a water feature and calls the result a garden.

Here in Cornwall I reckon that we've got more proper gardeners than we've a right to, and that while some television gardening programmes these days are encouraging us to go for the "instant" garden there are still enough people left who are sensible enough to know that the best gardens certainly aren't the instant variety and who are putting in plants today that won't be at their best for another fifty or one hundred years. Anyone who's ever walked around some of the big Cornish gardens and seen the huge magnolias, rhododendrons and soaring palm and pine trees is reaping the benefit of work carried out long before they were even born.

I'm sure that you've got your own favourite Cornish garden just as I've got mine. Trelissick, Trebah, Caerhays, Glendurgan, Trewithen, Lanhydrock - the list could go on and on. It's hard to know just who were the first Cornish gardeners though; they tell me that archaeologists found illustrations of plants on the wall plaster of Cornwall's only Roman villa near Camborne but to me it doesn't exactly prove that a toga-wearing Alan Titchmarsh lived there. Later the monks and holy men who built the important Cornish priories in the tenth and eleventh centuries certainly grew vegetables as well as medicinal herbs for themselves but it wasn't until Cornwall began to get rich through mining in the eighteenth century that the great gardening boom began. Back then the big estates of Carclew, Tehidy and Mount

Edgcumbe were the envy of the county for their elaborate designs and planting. I think that Cornwall's other great claim to fame as far as gardening is concerned is that many of the large estates were involved in plant hunting expeditions to China and the Far East at the turn of the century. This was when Cornish landowners such as J.C. Williams of Caerhays grew on rare specimens brought back by explorers such as Ernest Wilson and George Forrest. Together with the Lobb brothers - William and Thomas - from Egloshayle, they were the men who were responsible for present day gardeners like you and me being able to go along to the local garden centre and find what are now everyday plants such as *Magnolia Sinensis* and *Clematis Armandii*.

These days there aren't many wild corners of the world left to explore but there's still lots of work going on in Cornwall to develop new varieties of plants for everyone to enjoy. Take the humble daffodil for example. The late Barbara Fry from Camborne and currently Ron Scamp from Falmouth have both received international recognition for their specialist work in breeding new varieties of narcissi. I wanted to plant more daffs in my garden and so last summer I went to the Fentongollan bulb farm near Truro which Jim Hosking runs with his family. Over the years he's introduced a huge range of narcissi to the commercial market such as 'Knight of St John' and 'Princess Diana' and it's at this time of year when everything is still cold and wet and it's hard to even set foot in the garden at all that I'm very glad I did. The coming summer still seems a very long way  away but even this early in the year there are signs of life already - those Fentongollan bulbs pushed up through the soil right on cue and I've had different sorts of daffodils in flower since the day before New Year's Eve and a big sprawling camellia which I was given as a cutting (see what I mean about gardeners being nice people?) about fifteen years ago has been covered in deep pink flowers since before Christmas. Even in the rain it cheers you up just to take a glance at them as you hurry in through the front door to the fireside. I was reading in a magazine recently that an American clinical psychiatrist has been given a multi-million dollar grant for giving his patients pot plants rather than pills. He claims to have "discovered" that looking at the plants makes people happier than swallowing handfuls of tablets. Makes you wonder doesn't it?

...AND OVER THE GARDEN WALL

Despite what we might think on February days like this we're lucky in Cornwall to live in an area of the UK with a relatively mild climate. This means that we can grow

plants outdoors here which wouldn't survive elsewhere in the country. I was introduced to the idea of "exotic" gardening about fifteen years ago and I must say that from having just one or two small palm trees in pots one thing has led to another and now my garden is crammed with plants like tree ferns, bananas and those tall pointed echiums you see on the Isles of Scilly. When people first see the garden the first thing they normally say is "Wow!" just because everything is so lush and green and jungly although the second thing they say is "But there aren't any flowers!" They're absolutely right - well there are a few actually - but frankly I couldn't care less. Rows of bedding plants in garish colours which only live for a few months just aren't me I'm afraid. Those clever patterns of "carpet bedding" that parks departments do with huge numbers of geraniums and marigolds in the summer are all very well in a park but not in my garden thank you very much.

The other thing you won't find in my garden are hanging baskets. For my money they're far more trouble than they're worth. For one thing they're expensive to buy in the first place, even more expensive to fill as you always seem to need more plants than you think, and then they need watering at least a couple of times a day during the summer. They're awkward to hang, rock in the wind and even then they're only at their best for a couple of weeks or so. That's where my "green" garden really scores of course. Rather than colour which may be short lived, the size, shape and texture of both the leaves, and of these exotic plants themselves (they seem to be called "architectural" these days) give you something to look at every month of the year. Even now in February, when it's been below freezing at night, the rain is lashing down and a neighbour's rose bed looks like piles of dead twigs marooned in a puddle, there are still bronze leathery New Zealand flax leaves shooting seven or eight feet up into the sky like swords coming straight up out of the ground, bright green feathery palm trees, rustling black and red bamboos and spiky yellow striped agaves which are all growing away perfectly happily.

It seems such a shame to me that, on the whole, people in Cornwall don't take advantage of growing these so-called "tender" plants like this and stick to the boring "safe and sure" things like conifers and heathers. Gardeners in the past haven't been so scared of trying things out (just think of those huge Chusan palm trees at Trebah or the forest of tree ferns in the Heligan Jungle) and it would be great to think that as visitors to Cornwall travelled further and further West into the county there were exotic lilies, acanthus and daturas growing in council flower beds rather than the boring begonias you might find in the middle of Birmingham! I have to say at this point though that I'm full of admiration for Simon Miles, the man at Carrick District Council who's responsible for those fantastic huge Phoenix palms from the Canaries that you see on the traffic roundabout at the end of the Penryn bypass, as well as all the other exotic palms and succulents along Dracaena Avenue and on the smaller islands and town beds in Falmouth. Having them greet you as you come into the town really makes you feel as if you're arriving somewhere special.

But whether you're a convert to "exotic" gardening like me or have found that your particular bit of heaven on earth is maybe a fruit orchard or a border full of delphiniums there's sometimes no better way of spending a spring Saturday afternoon that taking a break from your own garden and pottering around someone else's plot. As well as all the Cornish National Trust gardens and the great Cornish estates which invite us to walk down their garden paths on a regular basis, over the past few years a number of private gardeners have been brave enough to allow the rest of us to take a look around as well. The National Gardens Scheme's famous "Yellow Book" in hand, every weekend from March to August hundreds of people set off to enjoy, compare, learn and enthuse about the work of fellow gardeners. And we're a pretty determined bunch let me tell you. In my garden visiting career I've seen people standing in pouring rain, blazing sun, and hail storms (even snow on one memorable occasion). Of course as well as admiring you also get the chance to criticise and say to yourself "Well, mine's better than that!" - after all, their compost heap could turn out to be as soggy and smelly as yours. Visiting other peoples' gardens also gives you the opportunity of being able to justify being nosy and peering around corners into places where perhaps you shouldn't. Shed doors must be opened, naturally, to see if their lawn mower's as rusty and battered as yours and of course you just have to look under the greenhouse staging to check out how many empty packets of slug pellets might have been abandoned there.

The quality of the teas and the toilets comes in for scrutiny too. Some hosts go to a lot of trouble and beg and borrow extra seats and tables for their visitors, pulling out all the stops to impress. In the queue for tea at one garden I was once offered the choice of "Indian, China, Ceylon or a bag?" but they needn't have bothered. The lady in front of me, having sipped her cup, turned to her friend and in a booming voice for all the world to hear declared "Well with tea like this they don't need weedkiller!". If you open your garden to the public you also run the risk of falling foul of the sneaky snipper - the cuttings taker. Apparently the culprits more often than not are innocent-looking little old ladies who come prepared with a pair of secateurs and a plastic bag tucked neatly away in their handbags. Peter Borlase the former Head Gardener at the National Trust's Lanhydrock House once told me that the problem is actually quite serious and that some of his plants had all but been cut away entirely. You can't help but smile though when you hear that one person with their hands full of cuttings, when they were challenged by one of the gardeners, said that they were just trying to help the Trust out as they thought that the plants could "do with a bit of pruning"!

Despite the odd lapse, I still reckon we gardeners are a pretty nice bunch of people but be warned, if I'm ever tempted to open *my* garden to public scrutiny I might ask you to bring your own thermos and I shall definitely make sure that the shed door remains very firmly locked!

FLYING THE FLAG ON ST PIRAN'S DAY
March

You say "Pray Sands" and I say "Prar Sands", You say "Lan-sin" and I say "Lawn-sun" - and a TV or radio presenter could well be forgiven for adding "Let's call the whole thing off!" particularly when you think that these two places are spelt differently yet again - "Praa Sands" and "Launceston". Pronunciation in a news bulletin is always a problem (Scandinavian tennis players' names are a particular minefield) but nowhere is it more acute than in somewhere like Cornwall where two lifelong next door neighbours can make the name of their village sound like two entirely different places.

It's very fitting then that Cornwall's patron saint, or more correctly the patron saint of tinners, can sound as if his name is 'St Perran', 'St Pirran' or 'St Pyran' depending on whether you come from Polgigga or Polperro, Mulfra or Mullion. Recently one man has been responsible for making sure that March 5th has become a date written in every Cornishman's diary and that the flag of St Piran (I'll stick with the middle ground, thank you very much!) - the white cross on a black background - flies from the flagpoles of as many houses and public buildings as possible. Howard Curnow is a one-man, but worldwide, promoter of Cornwall and the Cornish. He's organised gatherings of Cornish people across the globe, worn his tartan kilt from Camborne to Cuba and has made sure that St Piran's day has blossomed into an important annual event.

Driving across the single track tarmac lane that winds over the scrub and sand dunes toward the huge caravan and chalet holiday park just north of Perranporth (Piranporth? - please don't ask!) just about every car proudly claimed its Cornish identity; "Cornish Solidarity", "BBC Radio Cornwall" and "Kernow" stickers were plastered across windows, black and white flags fluttered from aerials and black and gold scarves trailed from windows. Not quite twenty thousand, but well over one thousand, "merry hearts and true" clambered from their cars, unfurled banners and flags and, with splashes of Cornish gold from gorse and daffodils, set off in one long vast procession snaking through the dunes led by (the Pied?) piper Mervyn Davey and his son Cas beating time on a drum.

The procession came to a halt as actor Michael Truscott appeared on the skyline dressed in monk's robes (black and white: how convenient!). This was Ciaran, a 5th century Irish holy man who was then promptly sent to his death - pushed over a handy dune masquerading as the cliff edge by a jealous king. The procession set off again, leaving the actors playing the local peasants to much wailing and gnashing of teeth. There was no time to worry about them now, though, for the leaders had reached a pond in a dip in the dunes. Here Ciaran (who, through a bit of linguistic jiggery pokery, was now known as Piran) and who had happily recovered from his fall was now rowing a coracle ashore in Cornwall carrying a holy stone.

Welcoming as ever, the Cornish took him in and helped built his first church. This part of the re-enactment took place on the actual site of the first Oratory and a later eighth century church - the site now sadly "lost" and buried in the sands. Eileen Carter who, if it wasn't for all the dunes in-between (as the song almost said) could see the Oratory from her home in nearby Rose, told me that the St Piran Project Trust had been campaigning for some time to have the church uncovered. Judging from her photographs and illustrations of previous excavations and work on the site, which she'd put on display for the marchers I, for one, think it would be well worth doing, although how you would ever find it without the trusty Mervyn piping you on your way is anyone's guess.

On again, past the Oratory, over the stream and up the hill to what Howard tells me is the "third" church - now in ruins but with a tall lichen covered carved granite cross alongside. Here, in brilliant sunshine, but clustered together against the biting wind, and with the flags snapping around our ears, we saw Piran discover the silver stream of tin flowing from the blackness of his hearth. This was the cue for much 6th century style merry making and, although you'd have thought he'd learned his lesson, St Piran falling to his death for the second time having had, shall we say, a drop too much, and instantly creating the expression "as drunk as a Perraner". Will Coleman (who'd directed much of the pageant) and his sister Hilary bought the Piran legend up to date and as everyone packed in around the Celtic cross for a stirring rendition of "Trelawny" our hero appeared from the dead yet again - outlined against a giant St Piran's flag. "If only Cornwall could come back to life as often as he did," was the comment from a man dressed head to toe in yellow and black tartan standing next to me.

It's true of course that, particularly in the last twenty years, there have been huge body blows to the Cornish economy. The county's three traditional industries - fishing, farming and mining - have all suffered and it was a sad day when I presented an outside broadcast programme from the gates of South Crofty on the day in 1998 that Cornwall's last working tin mine closed, the final crew coming to the surface from the seams four hundred fathoms below my feet. On the site wall someone had written in huge white letters "AND WHEN THE FISH AND TIN ARE GONE, WHAT ARE THE CORNISH BOYS TO DO?" and there was an enormous sense of despondency everywhere you turned.

But, as the wind whipped our words away across the shifting sand, my new tartan friend and I agreed that while the county would never see again the days of millions of pilchards being landed in a single day in Newlyn or thousands of men drilling ore from the ground there were some signs that, perhaps, the corner had been turned. Objective One funding, a University for Cornwall, the Tate Gallery- St Ives, the Eden Project - although so far only making a dent in the huge unemployment figures - could be showing us the way to go. We all felt we'd taken part in much more than a march. While it's true that there were now celebrations and picnics dotted in sheltered spots amongst the dunes, many people quietly left offerings of daffodils and gorse at the foot of the cross or on the Oratory and wandered back to their cars deep in thought. If a coracle came ashore today, what message for Cornwall would its sailor bring?

THE WESTERN HUNT POINT TO POINT
March

Have you ever seen the musical "My Fair Lady"? If you have I'll bet (providing I get good odds!) that you'll remember the "Ascot Gavotte" where Eliza and assorted members of the aristocracy spend a day at the races. Even though dukes and earls may have been a bit thin on the ground that Saturday, not to mention Cockney flower sellers, there's no denying that hundreds of Cornish people turned out for *their* day at the races at the Western Hunt's Point to Point meeting on the Royal Cornwall Showground. As we turned in through the gate our whole car load of grown ups, children and dogs was warmly greeted by the stewards like long lost friends and even though none of us had set foot on (or should that be "over"?) a horse for many years we were immediately made to feel part of what was going on. How many events do you go to which you can say that about?

As we walked down toward the course and the Royal Cornwall's huge cattle shed (which had been turned into a giant - but rather draughty - bookmakers for the day) you might have been forgiven for thinking you had come to a dog show rather than a horse race. Judging from the number of them around, a dog was obviously *de rigeur* for the occasion, and the sportier the better, as dozens of Labradors, Setters, Terriers and Jack Russells nosed their owners out of the way so that they could get a better view of the track for themselves. Just by chance, one of my friends had brought her spaniel with her and so with 'Blue' in tow, a race card, and a borrowed pair of binoculars we felt we looked the part, at least, as we waited for starter's orders.

The row of spectators at the trackside looked like a tideline of tweed as it snaked its way over the brow of the hill and down towards the finishing line. The green and brown was flecked with the bright orange of the stewards' tabards as they tried - mostly in vain - to stop the more over-eager racegoers from trying to cross the track. Next year the organisers could try hiring a few school crossing patrols to help out, although I don't think they'd stand as much chance of actually stopping a few tons of thundering horseflesh as they do with the school run Volvos with which they do daily gladiatorial combat.

One of the good things about the Wadebridge showground track is that it rises and falls over the countryside so that wherever you're standing you can get a view of at least part of the course but of course the finishing line attracted an excitable clot of people as the first winner of the afternoon shot past the post. The races are timed so that everyone can have a breather in-between each one and (in my case pretend to) study the form.

I must come clean and say that I know absolutely nothing about racing. As someone who failed his Maths 'O' level more times than I care to remember, working out the odds is a nightmare and race card notes such as "5pppO-1u" and "Left clear maiden, fair 3rd S. Pool, stays. Best fresh. gd." mean as much to me as a radio programme running order probably would to Frankie Dettori. Undaunted though we hung over the rail of the paddock and nodded, pointed, whispered and scribbled on the racecard along with everyone else. Using this simple formula and basically deciding which of them we liked the look of (although even I had to reject a friend's suggestion of one horse, based purely on the fact that the jockey's colours matched her new dining room curtains!) we decided on our own favourites.

It's all supposed to be a bit seedy, though, isn't it - gambling? Many people must have a mental image of Flash Harry the spiv played by George Cole in the St Trinians films of the 1950s when they think of life behind the multi-coloured plastic strip curtains of the average High Street bookmakers but, here on the showground nothing could have been further from the truth. Sarah and Bob Baker are the joint secretaries of the Point to Point and they tell me that they have a huge cross-section of the public who turn up as regularly as clockwork - everyone from dedicated hunt supporters to families simply in search of a good day out. This year I noticed little elderly ladies in twinsets and pearls jostling to get the best odds

alongside teenagers dressed for the disco, young mums and dads, the odd country gent and (whisper it quietly) even one or two men of the cloth. They thronged around twelve bookmakers' stands arranged in a line across the floor of the cattle shed. The bookies seemed to be mostly local men - "Racing Roy Bolitho" and "George Edwards - Plymouth" proclaimed two of their hoardings - who stood on small sets of steps alongside the boards on which they wrote their odds. Traditional leather briefcases held their takings and behind each man stood a clerk busily scribbling down the bets one by one. Some serious money was being handed over but for most people that afternoon their wagers were just single pounds. Whatever the bet, the agonising over the decision over which horse to back and the dejection or elation after the race was no less keenly felt.

After four races and four £1.00 stakes my beginner's luck made sure that I was £3.50 up on the afternoon and so the teas and cakes were on me. Elsewhere I could have been tempted to part with my winnings by videos of past Point to Points (presumably made so that the winners could re-live their moment of glory on freeze frame again and again), a selection of horse tack or personalised photographs of winners of previous races that I could put on my mantelpiece. Somehow I managed to resist and we made our way back out onto the course.

The race commentator, perched on top of his scaffolding tower like a stork nesting on the top of a Mediterranean church tower, crackled and boomed across the field to make sure that wherever you were you knew what was going on, although for judges and a privileged few there was space to stand on a farm trailer - the equivalent of a Grandstand I suppose. Here a strict dress code seemed to be in force - this was the place for bowler hats, wax jackets and binoculars onto which had been tied dozens and dozens of race track members' passes so that they dangled and jangled like a dowager's charm bracelet. Not for the likes of us or indeed for the over-enthusiastic stable girls, identified by the head collars and bits of baler twine stuffed into their pockets and by the bits of straw clinging on to their padded jackets. They energetically jumped up and down, wobbly in too tight jodhpurs, screaming out the pet names for their particular charges as they galloped past. "My Little Pony" has a lot to answer for.

The day also gave everyone an opportunity to display all those tricksy sorts of portable seating you can buy these days from Sunday newspaper catalogues as families and friends pitched camp on the surrounding slopes for the afternoon. Trusty old shooting sticks, bearing the scars of years spent following the local hunt, lined up in the stalls next to posh teak fold up jobs (excellent form but no staying power). They favoured the going good to firm but those precarious little three legged collapsible stools - their tops a tiny triangle of green canvas - which would have liked it good to soft, inevitably deposited their owners onto the ground with monotonous regularity. (In fact we ran a book ourselves with odds as to how many times a lady, sitting in front of us and dressed head to foot in her best Jaeger, was unceremoniously dumped onto the grass by her unruly mount.) Picnic rugs put in a strong showing at the finish and the grass became splattered with plaid patches as the afternoon wore on.

After the final race, wins and losses were added up but, at the end of the day (you have to use that expression when you're talking about sporting events), it really didn't seem to matter much. Everyone seemed to have had a thoroughly good afternoon out regardless of their financial state. This was the happiest event I'd been to in a long time; racegoers are certainly a jolly lot, there were smiles everywhere as people headed home. I held my car door open for Clare, who's eight. "That was really good fun," she said. I agreed with her; Ascot had got nothing on Wadebridge.

A DAWN CHORUS AT HELIGAN
April

Well it was April Fool's Day after all.

On the face of it, it did seem like a foolish proposition - getting up at five o'clock in the morning to go and stand in the rain listening to a few birds singing. But there's nothing some people like more than a challenge and, instead of just turning over, ignoring the sound of the rain hammering on the bedroom window and going back to sleep, well over a hundred people from all over Cornwall gritted their collective teeth in the darkness and set off to hear the Dawn Chorus at the Lost Gardens of Heligan near Mevagissey.

Now when it comes to getting up early in the morning I reckon that I can teach most people a thing or two. When you're asked to present a breakfast programme on the radio or on the television, it's a bit of a doubled-edged sword. It's very nice to be asked, of course, but it does mean that your life is turned upside down. Your day begins at four o'clock in the morning and ends about eight o'clock at night. Over the years I've adopted a system of three alarm clocks to make sure I don't oversleep. The first one is electric with illuminated digits so that I can read the time in the dark on the countless occasions when I wake up about eleven o'clock in the evening thinking I've overslept. The second is a battery-powered standby in case there's a power cut in the night and the third and final one is on the other side of the room so that I physically have to get out of bed to turn it off and am not tempted just to fling out a hand to silence the other two and go back to sleep. After all it would never do for the person to whom so many people say "Oh, you're the person who wakes me up in bed every morning!" to have to be woken up himself!

Being organised is everything. I read an interview once with breakfast TV presenter Penny Smith in which she said that every night she laid a trail of a banana, yoghurt and so on down her staircase to pick up for her breakfast as she hurtled out of the door. At that time in the morning you certainly don't feel like making a few sandwiches for lunch, leisurely mashing (sorry, Midlands roots showing!) a pot of tea or spending a few minutes looking at the weather and deciding what you're going to wear. In any event crashing around the house switching the lights on wouldn't be popular with anyone else trying to sleep. The routine is that it's out of bed and into and out of the shower in four and a half minutes flat. Then shave, dress in clothes laid out the night before, gulp down a glass of fruit juice and a handful of vitamin tablets and straight out of the front door picking up the coat, car keys and briefcase all left waiting overnight by the front door.

But no matter how strict you are about going to bed early, as any shift worker will tell you, getting up in the early hours every day for month after month does make you feel as if you have some sort of permanent jet lag. The bags under your eyes get darker week by week and you seem to be more susceptible to any bug that's doing the rounds. Lots of people say to me how miserable it must be getting up and going out early in the middle of winter when it's cold and dark and wet. But, perversely, I find the summer a lot harder to cope with. Yes, it's not quite as bad getting up when it's getting lighter and the weather's a bit warmer, but at four in the morning it's never *that* light and it's never *that* warm. But worse, much worse, is trying to get to sleep at eight o'clock in the evening when the sun's still shining through the bedroom curtains and the noise of your next door neighbour's lawn mower comes through the open window along with the appetising smell of a nearby barbecue just getting under way. No, give me the winter months, anytime, when you can be warm and snug as the rain lashes against the windows in the darkness.

Penny Smith says that it's a case of 'phone off, TV off, door shut and ear plugs in and I must say it's a similar story for me. Friends get used to the fact that you can never go out for a drink with them in the evenings and colleagues know better than to ask you about a post-watershed TV programme or an item on last night's news. Sad isn't it? But there are compensations. Yes, there are, but I need advance notice before I can think of any of them. Except, of course, that having had an extra hour in bed that day *I* was the one looking bright eyed and bushy tailed at six in the morning in the car park at Heligan Gardens while other people were emerging yawning from their cars blinking themselves awake.

Everyone peered through the darkness as they put on walking boots and extra layers of clothing lit by the glare from their cars' interior lights as it spilled out of

doors and hatchbacks showing up the drifts of fine drizzle wafting through the trees. The dampness did make the air smell wonderfully fresh but what were we all thinking of? We could have heard a few blackbirds in our own gardens!

As more and more people arrived (were we *all* April fools?) the crowd sheltering inside the tea room grew bigger and bigger until Candy Smit, who organises the Friends of Heligan group which was behind the event, welcomed us all and explained that there were three guides to show us around or that, if we preferred, we could wander off on our own. By now everyone was eager to be off as it was getting lighter by the minute and the shapes of the huge trees and shrubs of the garden were forming out of whatever you call the morning equivalent of the gloaming. We attached ourselves to David Hastilow's group and set off down the drive. David is a freelance photographer and ornithologist, who's been involved with the restoration project at the gardens for years. Softly spoken, with his boots and camouflage jacket, David immediately struck us as the sort of man who knew enough about nature to make a fire, build a shelter and cook a three course meal in the middle of a forest armed only with a penknife and a piece of string. We were in safe hands.

Carefully trying not to make any more noise than we could, we set off down the main drive in his footsteps, for all the world like safari tourists following David Attenborough through the African bush. We paused every few yards while David looked about him and listened for squeaks and cheeps and whistles. Within a few yards of the main gate we were already able to tick several species off our "hit list" - seagulls and rooks of course, along with black caps, robins and chiffchaffs. Pretty soon we'd added a lot more - blue tits, pigeons, blackbirds and both green and greater spotted woodpeckers. David was a veritable mine of information. He explained how we could build up an accurate picture of bird life in any given area without actually seeing a single feather, but merely by listening and plotting the position of the calls we heard

and that people who are blind or who have sight problems can easily become bird "watchers" too. He also told us that birds sing in a form of dialect which helps them find their way back to exactly the same place year after year (imagine all those elegant superior-looking swallows which visit Cornwall every summer saying to each other "proper job me 'ansomes, 'tis fitty to be 'ome"!) and that robins are so territorial (but obviously terribly short sighted) that they'll attack a perfectly innocent red tomato if you put one on your lawn because they see it as a threat. I tried it when I got home; they do too!

The success of the Lost Gardens of Heligan has been phenomenal. Helped by a popular Channel Four television series and a best selling book written by the

garden's driving force Tim Smit, millions of visitors have been able to trace the gradual reclamation of the various parts of what was once a thriving estate. What makes visiting the garden special for me, and for many other people, is the fact that it's easy to trace the personal stories of the men and women who lived and worked there. Photographs of "the gunnera man", a Victorian gardener proudly holding aloft a so-called "giant rhubarb" leaf, and the names of the men scratched into the plaster in the "thunder box" room mean that present day visitors can easily imagine the estate in its bustling, but ordered, prime in those fragile years just before the outbreak of the First World War. Conscription meant that the estate was no longer viable and it was left to decay until Tim and his colleague John Willis hacked their way through the undergrowth to discover - and eventually reawaken - their own "Sleeping Beauty".

One of the other attractions of Heligan is that it has once again become very much a working garden. There can't be many people in the country - let alone Cornwall - who haven't heard of their attempts to grow pineapples in pits heated by decomposing manure. The marshalled rows of fruit and veg in the kitchen garden would do Peter Rabbit's Mr McGregor more than justice and the espalier fruit trees wired and pinned to the walls of the melon garden are a tribute to the art of the pruner. In other words there's a lot more to see than just some pretty flower beds and people come back again and again to check on the progress of their favourite plants. They feel very proprietorial about them too - after all there aren't many individual gardens with a "fan club" of getting on for 2,000 people - and even while we were there early that morning a fellow Friend of Heligan excused himself from the rigours of our high-intensity nature ramble to check on the progress of some citrus trees to which he was apparently closely attached. Or perhaps he just couldn't stand the pace.

By now we were in the lowest "jungle" part of the garden and David had "tuned us in" to the sounds all around us as - with full daylight - squeaks, squawks, shrieks, chirrups, tweets and warbles seemed to be coming at us thick and fast through the dripping undergrowth. We stopped and sniffed the characteristic rank smell as David froze in his tracks to show us where a fox had shared our path, and nodded at each other knowledgeably at the sight of tufts of badger hair caught on the lowest strand of a barbed wire fence. We began our hike back on the boardwalk on the opposite side of the valley. For many people the Heligan Jungle is one of the most atmospheric areas of the garden with its primeval swampy floor and towering palms, bamboos and tree ferns swaying over our heads. And, despite my earlier doubts, this was the perfect time of day to see it as the mist hung over the stream and the ponds but shafts of light cut through the overhanging branches. Beautiful though it was hunger called us on. Back we traipsed, still following David in our safari crocodile, but now listening carefully for ourselves with me, for one, smugly tracing the sound of what I now knew to be a blackcap as it flew alongside us back towards the garden entrance. Waiting for us was a Cornish breakfast of bacon and sausage from Heligan's pigs, with Heligan produced eggs and honey. Everyone was ravenous; all that listening makes you hungry, and I'll bet even David Attenborough never gets a better breakfast!

SPENDING A WEEKEND ON SCILLY
April

Islands are pretty magical places, aren't they? There are treasure islands, islands of dreams and desert islands (some even complete with discs). They can come "full of noises that give delight" or even "sceptred" and here in Cornwall we've got a whole lot of them right here on our doorstep. They're called the Isles of Scilly or just Scilly (but absolutely not the Scilly Isles, thank you very much) and there are hundreds of them. The vast majority are simply bits of rock which emerge from the water for an hour or so every low tide but their five biggest inhabited cousins - St Mary's, Tresco, St Martin's, Bryher and St Agnes - are so special that they manage to attract thousands of visitors every year.

Just as Cornwall isn't England, so Scilly isn't Cornwall and, as a result, even though you might live on the mainland only about thirty miles away, going over there really does feel like going on holiday. I know some Cornish people who wouldn't dream of visiting anywhere else and others for whom even a day trip is looked back on fondly for years afterwards. So what is it that makes them so special or "fortunate" as they call themselves?

Many people tell me it's that Scilly is like Cornwall was years ago - traffic-free streets, a lack of crime and a slower pace of life. Incidentally, there's a lovely but alas, I think, apocryphal story which I've now heard told about shops on each of the islands which goes like this:

> Visitor: Have you got the Sunday Telegraph?
> Shopkeeper: Today's?
> Visitor: Yes, of course!
> Shopkeeper: Then come back tomorrow.

It's certainly true that the laid back way of doing things has its attractions but, for me, Scilly has far more than that. Each of the islands has its own character and, if the tide lets you time your boat trips properly, I reckon that in a weekend you can just about sample them all. In two days you might not have time for the uninhabited ones too, but the seals, puffins, gannets and gulls which live on Annet and the Eastern Isles will be there when you come back. And you will, mark my words.

My introduction to St Mary's was many years ago when I went with my parents and my brother on a day trip on board the Scillonian. The sea was rough and the journey took considerably longer than it should have done so that by the time we docked on the quay at Hugh Town we were all looking like one of the shades on a "white with a hint of green" paint colour chart. It was then that it started to pour with rain and we spent most of our time wandering from cafe to cafe trying to keep warm. Through the rain I could just about see hints of sandy beaches, flowers and huge rocks and even though the weather didn't let up until after we'd arrived back in Penzance that evening I'd already decided I'd be back.

The next time the weather was kinder, and from St Mary's I took a boat across what was, to me, a surprisingly blue and flat stretch of water (was this the same place? I asked myself) to St Agnes to record a radio programme with Sue Hicks the cookery writer and broadcaster. At that time Sue lived in what must be just about one of the most westerly houses in the UK and the view of the sunsets from her garden  would have kept scene painters from "South Pacific" in business for weeks. She'd had just finished presenting "The Fish Course" series for BBC2, but had been working before that on "Pebble Mill At One" which was a live programme and involved several hair-raising trips from the island to the studios in Birmingham via boat, helicopter, train and taxi carrying Scillonian vegetables and flowers and even freshly caught lobsters thrashing about in a wicker basket! Nowadays e-mail, video links and the internet have brought many more opportunities but Sue must have been one of the first people to prove that you can live in the place you love, either on Scilly or in the remoter parts of Cornwall, and still earn a living up country. For me St Agnes is the most romantic of the islands. Joined to Gugh by a narrow strip of sand, which is covered at high tide, it's as far west as you can go before you reach the USA. There's always been something about "heading west" that's attracted dreamers. America's Pacific coast, like Cornwall, is full of artists and adventurers and this island, with its tiny stone Troytown Maze, the Beady Pool where glass treasures from a seventeenth century Dutch ship are discovered in the sand and the sentinel Old Man of Gugh, is as dreamlike as they come.

Sailing in the other direction from St Mary's you arrive at St Martin's. You can forget the Caribbean - this island has some of the most spectacular beaches in the world. It's long and thin and hilly and with relatively few people living there - you'd be forgiven for walking from Lower Town, through Middle Town to Higher Town without realising you'd been in a town at all! Life on Scilly has always been hard but it's on the off-islands that people have to be able to turn their hand to a variety of jobs to make a living and where traditions are particularly important. Heather Terry who teaches in the island's tiny primary school says that her school admissions book contains the names of entire families - generation after generation after generation. She even went to the school herself and says that she was fortunate that after a spell away she was able to come back to work here. There are fewer than ten children at the St Martin's school at the moment and - like younger children from the other off islands - after they reach the age of eleven they go to board at the secondary school on St Mary's which despite (or should that be because of) its isolation consistently tops the government's various league tables.

I always associate Bryher with storms. Now, don't misunderstand me, I'm sure that the weather on Bryher can be as calm and sunny as on any of the other islands but whenever I've been there the wind's been blowing so hard it's difficult to stand

upright. It's when you experience the fury of an Atlantic gale which hasn't had anything in its way for a thousand miles or so until it reaches you that you realise quite how tough conditions have been for islanders over the years. It's particularly poignant to look across from Bryher to the derelict cottages of the once-inhabited island of Samson and think of the lives that were once lived there. There's a story that over half Samson's population was lost in a single night just after the turn of the nineteenth century when nineteen men drowned when their gigs foundered on Wolf Rock off Land's End. The community never recovered. The last crofters to leave did so in 1855, closing their front doors and crossing the water to St Mary's for the final time. Now though, leaning back into the wind and looking out over Hell Bay as the breakers crash against the Mussel Rocks and Shipman Head, it's good to know that there's a cosy B&B to go back to. But if you fancy something a bit more sophisticated than a B&B then you should head for Tresco and the Island Hotel.

Just over 150 years ago Augustus Smith came to what was a fairly bleak and inhospitable island where, like the other off-islands, in the early years it must have been a struggle just to survive. Nowadays however champagne and lobster are on the menu at the hotel, the silver's polished and the linen starched. Far from a starchy atmosphere though as bare feet sprinkling sparkling white sand behind them patter through reception and mums and dads and kids with a clutter of crab nets and kites pile on board the tractor which takes guests to and from the heliport. Tresco has its very own helicopter service to and from Penzance. The journey's quick (only about twenty minutes) but it is noisy and, even though I've done it several times, as the helicopter takes off for its return journey and the gulls flock back on to the landing field, the silence that settles around you is still one of my favourite moments there. This is a heliport with a difference. "Terminal One" is a wooden pavilion in the Abbey Garden and isn't the man who's issued your boarding card the same one who was taking cuttings in a greenhouse earlier on? On Tresco you find that, more often that not, people "double up" on jobs too, and even Mike Nelhams, the Curator of the Abbey Garden, also works at the heliport and is one of the island's trained fire-fighters!

Of course, it's the Abbey Garden that most people come to see. Begun way back by Augustus Smith, successive generations of the Dorrien-Smith family have played their part in developing and extending the plant collection. If you had thin sandy soil in your garden, like Mike and his staff do in theirs, then you'd be off to the garden centre for a sack of Multipurpose in no time at all, but, because of Scilly's mild climate and the extra shelter belt which the garden has, plants grow outdoors here that would barely survive in a greenhouse elsewhere in the UK. There are plants from Africa and South America, from Australia, the Canaries and New Zealand and the place is now so famous that visitors come from all those countries, and a good few more, to take a look at them. Indeed, these days it's quite common to see a huge cruise liner anchored off the island - her passengers coming ashore to marvel at just what's growing there.

Tresco's present owner, Robert Dorrien-Smith, has made his mark in the garden too. The snows of 1987 and the hurricane of 1990 meant that in three years the garden suffered more damage than in the past hundred and was all but destroyed. I went there in the spring of 1990 and walking amongst the uprooted remains of some of the ancient cypress trees which had once provided shelter for rare species to grow beneath them - those same species which now lay exposed and frosted - I met a woman in tears. She told me that she had been coming to Tresco for the past twenty years at that time every year and she believed that the place she loved would never recover. "It's too much," she told me. "The garden's finished. I can never come here again." Well, all I can say is that I hope she *has* gone back since because, with support from Robert Dorrien-Smith, Mike Nelhams and his team have not only re-created the garden but re-designed sections with extra planting to make it better able to cope with any freak weather conditions in the future. They've also added new features such as a Mediterranean garden complete with ancient olive trees and an exquisite shell house, designed and made by Robert's wife Lucy. Paradise has been regained.

So, all in all, I'd trade two weeks on the *costas* for a weekend on the Isles of Scilly any day and judging from the "no vacancies" signs in hotel and cottage windows so would a lot of other people. Whether I could live there or not is another question; I think you have to be a very special sort of person to spend all your time on a small bit of rock in the middle of the sea. But while there are boats and planes and helicopters then I shall be Scilly's number one fan.

MAY DAY IN PADSTOW
May

It was the 'obby 'oss that did it.

Back in 1976 I'd applied for a teaching job in Cornwall and an interview had been fixed for May 2nd. There were other interviews to come in other parts of the South-west over the next few weeks; at this point this one was nothing special. Now I have to confess that up until then I had never been to Cornwall in my life - not even a day trip to Newquay - and so I decided to travel down the day beforehand and take a look at the place to see if I wanted to live there. So it was quite by chance that I happened to stumble on Padstow's traditional May Day festivities complete with the famous 'osses.

It was one of those brilliantly bright and sunny Cornish spring days with crystal clear visibility from the harbour over the estuary to Rock and the hills beyond. The branches of sycamore and laurel which decorated the streets were still fresh and green and a stiff breeze fluttered the bunting and decorations on the maypole in Broad Street. But what literally stopped me in my tracks were the enormous numbers of cowslips and tulips bound to the pole itself. Their colour was so intense in the sunshine, and the flower heads were tied so tightly with no stalks visible, that the length of the pole seemed to shimmer with red and yellow against the blue of the sky.

But it wasn't just a visual assault on the senses that morning. The drum beat which hammers out the traditional Mayers' song all day long is something which still has, for me, all these years later, some sort of primal physical force behind it. It is so insistent that you feel it inside you in the pit of your stomach as it compels people to follow its call. The moment, after the 'quiet' verse of the May song, when the beat begins again as the 'oss rises from the floor is quite magical.

I stood there in Padstow on May morning in 1976 quite entranced; abandoned my plans of touring the rest of the county on the spot and stayed in the town for the entire day making friendships which still remain and vowed that if I was offered the job the following morning then I'd take it like a shot. I was, and I did.

Since 1976 I've been back to celebrate May Day in Padstow every year, and being there on May 1st has become virtually as important to me as family birthdays and Christmas. I've noticed that through the years the event has changed its character, though, and of course it varies from year to year depending on the weather and the people taking part. These days, with greater publicity, more and more visitors each year seem to go along and though I'm not one to talk, of course, thousands of people coming from outside the town can swamp things a bit. I remember years ago as the crowd surged to follow one of the 'osses through a narrow street one elderly lady called out "Padstow first, foreigners second" which, despite it not being entirely politically correct, I think in this case is fair enough.

Highlights for me since I first went have included watching the blue 'oss dance with Elizabeth Prideaux-Brune inside Prideaux Place, Padstow's great manor, from a vantage point halfway up the hall's sweeping staircase. Indoors the music seemed especially loud and the drumbeats rang in my ears for hours afterwards. For me the 'oss is too boisterous to be confined inside though; it was like watching a wild animal trapped in a cage and it seemed to leap with extra excitement as it burst back out through the front door into the sunshine.

Other particularly special occasions have included going along to the night singing. This takes place on the night before May Day and is altogether a much more sombre (though not sober) affair without the 'osses and the drums. It's the time for traditional folk music enthusiasts as midnight and the coming of the new May Day is welcomed with unaccompanied voices in the darkness of the streets.
On one of the nights I went along it poured with rain; thick heavy rain that soaked everyone, but it's a mark of how dedicated Padstonians are to keeping the tradition alive that water streamed down peoples' faces, making them shine in the lamplight, as the singing continued as loudly and as strongly as ever. But for me, every year virtually without exception, the highlight of the day has been the farewell, the moment when the blue 'oss returns to its "stable" in the Institute for another year. Despite the excitement and excesses of the day and no matter how wilted the town's greenery or the number of fish and chip wrappers in the street the one moment when the crowd sings its final unaccompanied "farewell" to the 'oss is always particularly poignant. One year I remember everyone was hushed to allow one elderly lady to sing alone. As her thin, small voice shakily followed the melody - as it had learned to do well over three score years and ten ago - I looked up to the bunting flapping and gently glowing in the last rays of the sun against the evening sky. Summer really had a'come that day.

...AND OTHER VISITS

Of course whereas in years gone by when people thought of Padstow they thought only of May Day, nowadays when you say "Padstow" to people (particularly from up country) they say "Rick Stein". As Noel Coward almost said it's extraordinary how potent television is. It seemed that, on the strength of one TV series "A Taste of the Sea" that Rick made in 1995, he (and Chalky his Jack Russell terrier, of course) suddenly became household names and that the world and his wife were queuing up to eat at his Seafood Restaurant. I found an old "Radio Times" photograph the other day of Rick and me (both looking slightly nervous and considerably younger it has to be said) which was taken to publicise a radio

programme I recorded with him, way before that first TV series was a twinkle in a director's camera lens. Back then the magazine's Editor asked why I was making a programme about a man who'd converted a disco into a fish restaurant. Now the cult of the TV celebrity chef means that a souvenir from Padstow these days probably means a Rick Stein recipe book rather than a stick of rock. Talking to Rick recently it's clear to me that while these days the world may roll over and wave its legs in the air (like Chalky on a heap of seaweed on the beach) when it meets Rick Stein, the opposite is certainly not the case. He's exactly the same down to earth chap (who also happens to be a brilliant cook) that he always has been. In fact I think it's his total lack of pretension (unlike some of his fellow TV celeb chefs, perhaps?) which makes him, and his other series "Fruits of the Sea", "Seafood Odyssey" and "The Seafood Lovers' Guide to Great Britain and Ireland", so popular. Years ago, travelling around the world, he once cooked for the navvies working on the old Afghan railway between Alice Springs and Adelaide and anyone who can do that and live to tell the tale must be pretty much fair dinkum.

It also his genuine enthusiasm for food and how it's cooked that's prompted the opening of his Seafood School. As somebody who doesn't know the difference between a gurnard and a grouper, much less how to cook them, I seized the chance to go along and have a look around. The school is on the first floor of a series of former fish sheds with wonderful views right out over the Camel estuary. In fact the views are so spectacular it would take me all my time to concentrate on what was going on inside rather than outside! Head Chef here is Paul Sellars who presides over ten small, but perfectly formed, mini-kitchens all set within one huge room. There's a demonstration unit at one end and an enormous pine table (made in nearby St Merryn) surrounded by sixteen chairs all with suitably fishily decorated cushions at the other. There's an interesting collection of antique plates and shelf after shelf of cookery books through which to browse. With a series of "porthole" windows, lots of blue and white paint and a curved panelled ceiling reminiscent of the sails of a schooner there's a nautical theme to the room but the teaching kitchens themselves are a world away from your average galley. Each of them is equipped with state of the art equipment, everything you'd need - and more - from an oyster shucker upwards. Each student has a set of professional kitchen knives too but, despite the warnings, many students simply don't realise quite how sharp they are. Good to know, then, that the blue first aid plasters, which I'm told sometimes have to be handed out like Smarties, blend in with the room's colour scheme!

Lots of fresh flowers and bleached wood welcome the school's students and when I went along, a group of "ladies who lunch" mingled with pensioners, a City businessman, a "foodie" husband and wife and some young, eager catering students, as they watched Paul's impressive demonstration classes before having a go themselves. The courses revolve around lunch - cooking it and eating it - and blenders whizzed, knives chopped and griddles fizzed faster and faster as everyone tried to put into practice what they'd learned that morning. If you want a top-notch cookery school in a place where you can virtually reach out of the window for a fresh fish then this is it. It was strange then, that despite the equipment, the building, the tuition and the food, one of the ladies who'd flown to Cornwall from London especially for the course confided to me that what she'd enjoyed the most was the opportunity of meeting "a real fisherman" on the quay!

It's also a strange thing that, in this country, while who dares *might* win, once they *have* won some of us don't half enjoy trying to knock them down again. "Padstein", a "foodie theme park", "Steinsville" are just some of the sneering comments about the town that critics have used to take a pop at the man who brings hundreds of thousands of pounds into the local economy every year. I reckon that what many people fail to see is that it's not just Rick Stein's restaurant or cafe that visitors spend money in and that nowadays, virtually whenever you go there, Padstow's car parks are full of enthusiastic visitors.

The last time I went there two ladies from a day trip coach tour came to stand beside me as I sheltered from the chilly autumn drizzle under a shop awning. Both were in their sixties with transparent plastic rainhoods pulled down over tight perms. Layers of white cardigans and quilted anoraks and zipped up fur lined ankle boots were trying to keep out the cold. We nodded to each other and I said - talking about the weather, as you have to do on such occasions - that they were very brave come to Padstow on a day like that. "Oh!" one of them said, "We wouldn't have missed this for the world. We wanted to see where Chalky lived!" There they were. Two people who had absolutely no intention of eating in Rick Stein's restaurant but who wanted to see the place that the man they knew from the television had talked about. Earlier on they'd had coffee then bought their lunch in a pub, taken a taxi up to Prideaux Place, gone shopping in the town, and were just about to get an ice cream and some sweets to eat in the coach as they travelled back to Torquay where they were staying. Not only had they spent money (and quite a bit of it) in the town, but they were taking away happy memories of a place they, in turn, would tell other people about. And there were fifty others on the bus just like them.

Harbour Master Captain Trevor Platt tells me that he's certainly seeing greater numbers of visitors than ever before come to the town - lots of them arriving by sea. The harbour berths have always been fully booked around May Day but these days yachts are rafted up alongside one another more and more often. There's a new brochure to welcome leisure sailors to the harbour and the town and the Harbour Commissioners were kind enough to invite me to open their new harbour office building which - along with a welcome - also offers all the practical facilities you need ashore after you've spent any time at all afloat. (A friend of mine once crewed on a yacht from Greece back to Falmouth and tells me she never thought she'd be so pleased to see a washing machine and a loo which flushed properly as she was when she arrived home!) It's a very smart, very Cornish building right on the harbour's edge - with traditional granite and slate on the outside - but inside there's all the latest technical equipment to enable Trevor and his colleagues to keep an eye on the comings and goings up and down the estuary. These days the water is very busy not only with fishing boats, the summer ferries and with yachts but with dozens of dinghies and sailboards setting off from Rock on the opposite bank. One of the commissioners joked with me that at times the water's so crowded you can almost walk between the decks from shore to shore without getting your feet wet! On the May evening of the opening - just like all those years ago when I'd first come to the town - the sun shone brilliantly and I ceremonially opened the front door, unveiled the plaque (on which another commissioner equally jokingly told me they'd spelt my name wrongly - they like a laugh in Padstow, apparently), and declared the building well and truly open.

The celebrations spilled out onto the quayside and standing in the evening sunshine I thought back to my first May Day; Padstow had lost none of its magic at all.

HELSTON FLORA DAY
May

There's a big red ring around the date of May 8th on every Helstonian's calendar - whether they live in that "quaint old Cornish town" itself or on the other side of the world. For those people who were born there, Flora Day is Christmas and birthday and Easter all rolled into one, so when you go along yourself, just after six o'clock in the morning, and walk through the streets towards the Guildhall with the bells of St Michael's ringing out, you can't help but catch some of the excitement that's in the air.

I'd made sure of a good vantage point on the corner of Meneage Street but this year the crowd was so dense I found myself sharing my square foot of pavement with several others including two backpackers whose rucksacks bulged with sleeping bags, saucepans and a camping stove. I asked them where they'd come from expecting, perhaps, that they were making their way around the coastal path. One of them explained that her great grandfather had been a "Cousin Jack" and had left Helston with four of his friends over a hundred years ago to work the mines in South Africa. The story of Flora Day had been passed down through the family and this year she and her boyfriend had travelled the thousands of miles back to the place the family still thought of as "home" to see what it was all about.

As she was telling me how her grandfather had always regretted not being able to come back to Cornwall again in his lifetime, a pair of red faced and flustered dancers, now dangerously late and near missing their famous on-the-hour start, skittered down the hill dodging policemen and balloon sellers and, much to their embarrassment, flung themselves into the Guildhall to the cheers of the crowd. Everyone's eyes began to turn to the clock. Less than a minute to go now. And then suddenly - as if we hadn't been expecting it at all - everyone jumped as Billy Pethick laid into his big bass drum with the first beats of the day. The dancers poured out of the hall in a seemingly never ending stream and squeezed their way between the lines of onlookers up the street heading for the top of Furry Way.

Although the sun wasn't shining it was bright and very humid and when some of the leading couples came back towards me one or two of them were looking decidedly hot and bothered. Several of the men's white shirt buttons strained across portly tummies and one or two of the ladies could easily have had "I wish I hadn't worn these shoes!" thought bubbles attached to their just-from-the-hairdresser perms. The route the couples dance is several miles long and remembering "walk, walk, hop, turn" for hours on end while trying to retain any sense of dignity as it grew warmer and warmer can't have been easy.

At this point I should say that if you're one of those people who always says "Furry Day" or "Faddy Day" or even "Feddy" or "Fiddy Day" then I'm sorry to make you wince every time I say "Flora". Don't blame me; that's what the Association asked me to call it years ago and I reckon they're the ones to know. One year a very irate radio listener wrote to me to say I should have called it "Floral Day" because of all the flowers that are worn. It was a well-known fact, he said. Insisted in fact. The letter went on to inform me that it had been called Floral Day years ago and this chap was going to start a campaign to reintroduce the name. You just can't win.

Of course there's more to Flora Day than just the dancing. I walked along to the Hal an Tow performance by St John's Bridge. It looks every inch like some sort of medieval mummers' play, and has English (rather than Cornish) roots, but is now an important part of Flora Day with St George and the dragon doing their thing, aided and abetted by a chorus including a traditional Green Man played by a bloke wearing lots of green make up and what looked like half a sycamore tree. There's nothing quite so whimsical about the dozens of "cheapjack" stalls which lined the streets down towards the Boating Lake. They were selling everything I never wanted from a potato peeler to a duvet cover with pictures of the characters from "Star Wars" on it - just the sort of thing to give you sleepless nights I would have thought. There were the usual crowds grouped around the stalls where salesmen were demonstrating gadgets for painting ceilings or peeling vegetables. Lots of people seemed keen to part with their money but I couldn't help wondering how soon these "wonder products" would be lying abandoned at the back of the kitchen drawer; I must say I've never been to anyone's house where they ate cucumber cut into long spirals like clever potato peelings, have you?

It was easy to think back to the Flora Days of years ago when instead of a plastic gizmo this same crowd's ancestors would have been snapping up the latest "patent" hair restorer or quack doctor's cure-all from the steps of a scarlet and gilt gypsy caravan. That same crowd might also have paid a farthing or two to a fortune-teller for reassurance about the harvest or news from the "other side". These ladies must be a hardy breed because - even in the twenty first century when you can download a personal horoscope from the internet -

they're still going strong. Judging from the queues their advice is as sought after as ever; there must be money in those crystal balls.

After dodging the dodgems and shying the coconuts it was back up the hill for the main event of the day, the Mid Day Dance. The Flora Day Association and Chief Steward Leslie Collins make sure that everything goes according to plan and no one steps out of line - and not just in their footwork either. For one thing we're talking dress code and then some. There hasn't been a morning suit available in any of Cornwall's dress hire shops for months and chaps who never even wear a tie from one week to another take to top hats and tails as if they were Fred Astaire. It's full-length formal gowns for the ladies - complete with hats and gloves. My fellow BBC Radio Cornwall presenter Tiffany Truscott has danced in the Mid Day Dance several times with both her father and brother, and tells me that the design and colour of the dresses is a closely guarded secret until the very last minute. Most of them are made especially for the occasion and apparently if you tell your fabric shop that the material is for a Flora dress they'll make sure that particular colour or design isn't sold to anyone else. There's also something called the "Flora style" to which all the ladies are supposed to adhere. Now, as a mere male, the finer points of this escape me, but over the years that I've been going to Flora Day, I've noticed that one or two of the designs which emerge from the Guildhall after twelve o'clock have been, shall we say, *unusual* as their wearers try to push back the boundaries of Flora fashion. This year, apart from one lady whose frock I could have sworn was made "Sound of Music" style from old brocade curtains - I thought that they all looked gorgeous, particularly another former colleague Rebecca Wills who, with her partner of the day Percy Tripp, led the Mid Day Dance in a blur of lilac satin as they set off from the Guildhall and (much to the consternation of a German lady standing by my side who thought the dancers had become disorientated!) headed straight into the electrical shop on the other side of the road!

Dancing in and out of shops and houses is all part of the day of course and it adds immeasurably to the character of the event. Tiffany tells me from personal experience that even though it's actually quite hard to do it's great fun. There's never enough room for the groups of four dancers to parade properly inside the buildings and there are inevitable bottlenecks as they go in and out of the doorways. So, while to you and me on the outside everything may look as if it's going smoothly, on the inside it can be a very different story - there are either too many people bunched up and squashed into someone's front room, or the leaders have gone through quickly and the ladies following behind have to hitch up their skirts and make a run for it from one door to another in an effort to close up a gap!

By the end of the last dance of the day the Helston Town Band can consider themselves well and truly "blown out", the lily of the valley is beginning to fade and some of the dancers are limping home to a hot bath and an urgent appointment with a tube of blister cream. But my Flora memory will be seeing a lady leaning out of the telephone box near the Guildhall, holding the receiver so that the person at the other end could hear the Band as they passed by. I spoke to her afterwards. "It was my sister in Canada," she said. "I haven't seen her in twenty years and we hardly keep in touch - just a card at Christmas - but I do this for her on Flora Day every year. However long she's in Canada, as long as she can hear the Band she'll always remember she's a Helston girl".

THE ROYAL CORNWALL SHOW
June

For many people in Cornwall the year revolves around the Royal Cornwall Show. The surrounding fields glint silver in the sunshine with row upon row of parked cars as hundreds of thousands of people pour on to the showground near Wadebridge. The three days of the show are a time for friendships to be renewed, deals done, rivalries challenged again in the show rings and for relations long since left Cornwall to come home and meet up with distant cousins over a cup of tea and a saffron bun in the WI tent.

My favourite time at the show is very early on the first morning. Everything is ready for the first visitors and there is a huge sense of anticipation and excitement. The dew is shaken off as tent flaps begin to open, and stockmen emerge bleary eyed from their wagons and make furtive expeditions to the shower blocks, towels and shaving kits in hand. Last minute adjustments are made to displays in the flower tent, champion dogs are given a final brush and the smell of frying bacon drifts across the show rings. This particular year a Royal visitor - in the person of Princess Alexandra - and good show-going weather (not too hot but dry underfoot) combined to make Show Secretary Chris Riddle walk around beaming under his bowler and to break attendance figures at well over one hundred and twelve thousand people. I always find the huge throngs who just amble along the main walkways and then pack the big trade marquees a bit daunting though. The real interest of going "up Royal" for me is being able to see into the working lives of other people. Obscure bits of specialist hi-tech farm machinery, displays of rabbit netting techniques or watching as the wood chips fly around the chair bodger all take me along the quieter backwaters.

This year my progress was halted by a procession of cattle being led from their stalls to one of the show rings. Craning to see the judging in progress my eye was initially caught not by the animals but by the judge. Willie McLaren, dressed in a vivid green kilt and tweed jacket, was making his way expertly up and down the line. Well respected throughout the cattle world, Mr McLaren had travelled from Auchterarder in Perthshire just to give his opinion on the line of beasts parading in front of him. The important title of Supreme Champion Beef Animal was at stake as the judge's eye and hands flickered across the powerful quarters noticing tiny imperfections invisible to the rest of us. The handlers tried to appear nonchalant about the whole thing but sidelong glances and pats of reassurance to their animals gave the game away. A decision. The red rosette went to the Aberdeen Angus Gaston Wood Georgina and an emotional Malcolm Williams from Manaccan. It would be a year to remember at Tregonwell Farm.

But I was on my way to see another breed. The previous year I had noticed the Belgian Blues for the first time. I think these animals are quite extraordinary. Extremely powerfully built, these cattle seem to have close cut hair, like a body builder shaving his chest, to give extra definition to each muscle. It also allows you to see the strange pinky blue colour of their skin. Chief Cattle Steward William Brent from Callington led me through the busy lines of animals undergoing the indignity of being washed and combed in their public dressing room stalls before making their appearance on stage. At the quieter far end of the shed were a dozen or so of the Blues. There were few people here and the air was still. Some of the

animals had a light covering of dust from the straw of the stalls, like gymnasts covering their hands with chalk, which only seemed to emphasise the strange luminous quality of their skin. Even though they lay relaxed, quietly chewing, their huge veined muscles still bulged and shifted under their weight and they looked for all the world like enormous marble statues which had begun to breathe. The prize-winning Belgian Blue Bull was named Roventon Oyster of the Stoneleigh Herd from Shebbear in Devon. He lay impassively in the soft creamy light which filtered through the canvas roof. He was quite magnificent and he knew it.

On my way back, outside the Members' Pavilion, I came across a little bit of Ye Olde Englande as horses and coaches were prepared for the coaching marathon. This year three teams were taking part. Each of the coaches had immaculate paintwork and was pulled by four horses with gleaming coats and polished harnesses and, with the odd bit of snow and a robin perched on the driver's brass coach horn, any of them could have driven straight off a Christmas card. The conditions of entry in the class insist that each coach has to carry no less than six people, including the driver, "servants" (the assistants who do all the really useful stuff like getting on and off to open gates and hold the horses), a representative of the showground and other passengers. All of them wear full period costume - frock coats and top hats for the men, and Victorian travelling capes, hats, veils and gloves for the ladies. No effort is spared to make sure that the image of each coach, its team and its occupants, is perfect. It came as a bit of a jolt then to notice that one of the ladies was wearing glasses. Not tiny, wire framed Victorian spectacles mind you, or even haughty lorgnette, but big, round, blue plastic frames. Somehow even her veil couldn't hide this twentieth century intrusion.

As well as being judged on their appearance the "marathon" part of this class is a sort of cross country journey the coaches have to undertake along the lanes near Wadebridge, and it was a popular choice when the black Gelderlander geldings Hugo, Hussaar, Gus and Earnest pulled Mark Broadbent's Red Rover coach into first place. They weren't the only ones to have to do some work, though, as Mark also won a prize for the best performance on a coaching horn. (I didn't hear him play myself but, apart from the post horn gallop, I somehow can't imagine that the coach horn repertoire is that extensive.)

It was a few years ago that I, along with some other BBC presenters, was offered the

opportunity of riding as a passenger in one of the coaches from that year's show marathon. Wisely, the coachman felt that our sartorial accomplishments wouldn't stand up to a judge's scrutiny and we arranged to meet some weeks later at his farm for a road marathon of our own. The four bay horses (complete with matching white blazes and socks) had been groomed especially for the occasion and seemingly endless yards of harness polished and soaped. The yellow and black coach had, I believe, once been a mail coach running to towns in Somerset and, with its red spoked wheels, had been lovingly restored. Having sat through rainy Saturday afternoon TV re-runs of "The Wicked Lady" with highwayman/woman Margaret Lockwood, or even American westerns such as "She Wore a Yellow Ribbon", I had always wanted to ride in a stage coach. What a wonderful way to travel, I'd thought. The chance to chat with fellow passengers, watch the scenery roll by, and all at a steady four horse power. I'd even imagined us, with Dalmatian dogs running behind, rolling up at a country tavern to be served by rosy cheeked wenches with goblets of ale. It was not to be. Six of us wedged ourselves into the benches inside the carriage, knees tucked under our chins and heads scraping the roof.

As soon as the horses moved off we realised why such a tight fit was important. The carriage's suspension (and I use the word loosely) was a series of leather straps and wooden laths which began to creak and groan. As the team broke into a trot, and later into a canter, we were thrown backwards and forwards against one another as the whole carriage lurched from side to side and back to front like a modern-day flight simulator. Precious little light came through the tiny four paned window and the noise of the hooves on the road and the grating of the iron-rimmed wheels drowned out any conversation. But the journey inside was nothing to that on the top. Climbing up the metal ladder at the rear you suddenly realise how high the whole contraption is off the ground. Sitting even higher than the driver, sorry, coachman, the backs of the horses seem very long way down and the road even further. The wooden bench seats are surrounded by a ridiculously low iron rail, to which you suddenly feel a great attachment as you begin to appreciate what a wonderful invention the seatbelt is. Of course the view over the hedgetops is terrific, though strangely only when you turn your face away from the driving rain, but it's certainly a useful distraction from the sparks which fly from the wheels when the brake is applied. In fact, going downhill in a coach is quite an art. The first time the coach servants clamber down from their seats, jump off and then run alongside the moving coach to try to guide the horses as their hooves slip and slide on the tarmac you begin to worry, but that's nothing to the terror you feel on the corners when it seems that the whole top-heavy contraption could turn over at any minute. I arrived back wet through, with white knuckles where I'd been clutching the rail, and a very numb backside. Years ago people would have thought little of crossing the entire country by mail coach. We had travelled just eight miles. So much for Olde Englande.

Back at this year's show sore feet and empty wallets told their own stories as pots of nodding fuschias and carrier bags full of "wonder" household cleaners and new-smelling waxed jackets made their way back to the car park. In the cattle lines the Belgian Blues ambled into their van to make their way home to Devon. Chris Riddle at last sat down for a cup of tea and the teams of riggers moved in to take down some of the stands. The sheep which normally live in these fields will be grazing here again in a few weeks. All over, for this year at least...I knew I should have gone to investigate that last marquee.

POINT AND PENPOLL REGATTA
June

One of the special things for me about a Cornish summer is to go along to some of the regattas which are held on the network of creeks and estuaries along the South coast. Each of them is special in its own way of course - Flushing, Port Navas, St Mawes, Percuil, Portscatho - but my favourite is at Point. More correctly called Point and Penpoll Regatta, the village shares its special day with the neighbouring village of Penpoll with which it merges, but with which it will never be merged! The villages lie downstream from Devoran near Truro and at one time were quite heavily industrialised with a railway, working quays and a lime kiln. Now, like so much of the south coast, the original cottages have been joined by some spectacularly ugly new holiday houses and bungalows but when you visit you still get a sense of it being a real working community.

Along with Devoran and Loe Beach, Point and Penpoll is one of a series of regattas held around the shores of Restronguet Creek. The pronunciation of the name of the creek is always a problem for tourists, and locals exchange smug looks when they hear "Restrongay", rather than the local "Restrongit". Point regatta relies on deep water to attract the larger boats and so the date varies from year to year according to the highest tides. This one fell in June, and unlike the past two or three years of either torrential rain or flat calm, the bright and breezy afternoon bought out quite a few people who set up camping chairs and picnic rugs on the quay.

The afternoon starts with Children's Sports, and what's more they're the sort of proper children's sports that I remember from my childhood - egg and spoon, three legged and sack races (with old fashioned hessian sacks). Point seems to be fortunate in that, unlike many small Cornish villages, it does have a number of young families, but nevertheless the opportunity of the Sports seems to draw children in from all over the area. Normally quiet mums become quite hysterical with excitement as their offspring totter toward the finishing tape, and dads mutter winning tips about egg balancing technique as they line up their youngsters at the start. The human racing, like the yacht racing, is all under the eagle eye of Officer-Of-The-Day Charles Warren who, with a practised hand, sorts the under-fives from the fives-and-overs, blows his whistle enthusiastically and with piercing effectiveness, commentates for the crowds, whose decision is Absolutely Final and yet who pulls the whole thing off with amazing good humour. After that a pause for breath and then it's down to the water.

Despite Charles's excellent commentary it's a difficult job to get any sense of what's going on when you're watching from the land at water level and certainly couldn't tell a centre board from a side board. After a while you might be able to sort the Toshers from the Optimists and the Sunbeams from the Shrimpers but, with the marker buoys some way off, and some even out of sight, I find it hard to know who's in the lead or even which boat is taking part in which race. The regatta programme offers helpful advice such as "the finishing line is the starting line crossed in the opposite direction" and "if a boat fails to return it will be disqualified" but I, for one, am none the wiser.

A miniature brass starting cannon signals the start of each race and cracks across the water as a tiny cloud of smoke whisks away and the spectators are forced to pause in their conversations and their picnics, while out on the water battles are fought to gain possession of the trophies named to honour local men and keep alive local surnames - Charlie Trebilcock, Reg Mitchell - a nice touch.

It's the appearance of the working boats which, as ever, proves to be the highlight of the afternoon. The depth of water at Point Quay means that these huge craft with their yards of canvas and polished heavy wooden masts, can be sailed, by an experienced helmsman, at some speed just a few feet from the spectators, turning at the very last moment. It's certainly close enough to hear the creak of their timbers and the slap of their sails and allow a tantalizing glimpse of life on board as they sweep up and then tack away. They're a real reminder of life on the water as it used to be here - no wonder their crews are rewarded with a WI tea in Graham Crocker's boathouse.

Point is *en fete* for the entire weekend. After the Saturday regatta and sports there's a service on the Quay on the Sunday morning and then sailboard events in the evening. The Monday evening sees a Watersports event where young children throw themselves enthusiastically into the water for swimming races under the gaze of watchful mums and dads. There are rowing events, running-and-rowing events (a sort of Point version of a decathlon) and Ran Dans and Sheaving competitions - neither of which I understand in the slightest.

Monday night is also Gig night. I think it's been amazing how quickly the number of villages and towns boasting their own gig has grown over the past ten years. One man who's kept the traditions of gig-making very much alive is Ralph Bird who lives nearby. Seeing him at work in his gig shed is a reminder of how boat-building was once a mainstay of life in this part of Cornwall. The gigs themselves celebrate the past too, with wonderful names like *Czar*, *William Peters* and *Dasher*. I think it's particularly good to see some of the junior teams power their way across the creek, with children learning the traditional skills of their fathers and grandfathers as they become at home on the water too.

A burger and hot dog stall keeps people warm enough on the waterside until the light begins to fade. Wet suit skins are shed and stuffed into carrier bags and boat trailers bump away down the Old Tram Road. On the Green the coloured bunting still flaps quietly and in the creek the curlews and oystercatchers reclaim their mudding feeding grounds as the tide ebbs away. Lights are burning now in cottages and houses as victories are celebrated and defeats explained away. There'll be scores to be settled next year.

A SUMMER'S DAY ON THE BEACH
July

It only happens once, or perhaps twice, a year.

It happens on a Saturday or Sunday so that you're not at work and when there are no shelves to put up in the back bedroom and when the lawn doesn't need cutting.

It happens in the summer when relations - whom you never see or hear of for the next eleven months - decide they can't come to stay in Cornwall after all. "All that traffic on the A30! All those people! How do you cope?" But most importantly it happens on the one or two days of July or August when you just know the sun is going to shine. A big round yellow blob has been stuck over Cornwall on the TV weather map for days and there's that warm, dusty sense of fullness and heat in the air which tells you that this is summer. It's the day when you can go to the beach.

I'm a big beach fan. I think it's something to do with being born right in the middle of England - virtually as far from salt water as you can get in any direction - that makes me enjoy just being on a beach virtually regardless of the weather. I also like the fact that a beach is a pretty special place - neither land nor sea but somewhere in-between - and maybe it's for this reason that over the years the idea of "the beach" has become a bit of a fantasy for lots of people. Film directors (remember Deborah Kerr and Burt Lancaster in "From Here To Eternity"?), advertising executives (would eating a "Bounty" bar be the same if it wasn't for the TV commercial?) and centuries of health "experts" have promoted beaches as places to fall in love, enjoy the good life or reap the benefits of sunshine, ozone and sea bathing.

Even in this country where, as we all know, the weather can be decidedly unfriendly, a whole tradition of beach going has grown up with bathing machines, piers, promenades and bathing beauties putting a seaside holiday into everyone's mind as some sort of panacea. It's a wonder the idea ever took off though. As far back as 1667 one Dr Robert White put forward seabathing at Scarborough (why Scarborough?!) as a therapy for all sorts of ailments including gout and worms. His advice didn't stop there though. He also told his patients to drink seawater too, slaked with milk! Despite all this, those seventeenth century beach-goers weren't put off and a book called "A History of Cold Bathing" went on to recommend a regular icy dip as a cure to "frail children, adolescent girls, shut-ins and urban dwellers". We may not be urban dwellers in Cornwall, but even today there are people who swim in the sea here every day throughout the year whatever the weather. One elderly lady, who takes to the water off Marazion every morning, told me that she'd "just got used to it". She said that she'd started when she was in her twenties but that she didn't really know why she did it any more. Maybe the chilly water had just frozen her little grey cells! She also reminded me that it was when she was a child in the 1920s that the fashion for sunbathing on the beach began and that the Mediterranean resorts of Cannes and Antibes had been full of bright young things anxious to achieve what was to become known as a "Chanel tan" after the fashion designer appeared in the resorts with a suntan in 1923. "Heliotherapy", as it was called, became an enormously popular pastime and "Sun Ray Health Resorts" were set up in the USA where "patients", supervised by nurses, lay in the sun on rows of beds all day long! Nowadays the dangers of sunburn are well known and even young children going to the beach in Cornwall are aware of the Factor number on their sunscreen. Planning a whole day on the beach involves more than suntan lotion though. You need to approach it like a military operation, particularly if you're taking children with you.

The first decision is where to go. Sand, shingle or rocks? Cliffs, dunes, or estuary? Coastal path, short stroll or nearby car park? Cafe and teashop or sandwiches and thermos? And where is the tide anyway? After that comes the "packing the beach bag" exercise. This involves rushing around the house grabbing swimming gear, towels, last year's paperback that you still haven't finished, a sandwich or two, bottles of water and a chocolate bar that you know will melt but decide to take anyway. On top of that there are the "optional extras" - chairs, windbreaks, kites, footballs. A quick head count to make sure everyone's there and out of the door.

Once you arrive you then have to go through the ritual of staking a claim on the particular patch of seaweed and sand that you then declare to be yours. Towels and coats along with buckets and spades set out at all four corners declare to the

world that this space is yours alone. If you've ever been on a beach abroad where huge noisy families come and plonk themselves down within a few inches of your towel, you'll know that this idea that a bit of the sand belongs to you is one unique to this country. Woe betide anyone who stakes a similar claim within a few feet.

Nothing will be said, of course, we are British after all. But there will be Looks. And if the offenders don't move on pretty sharpish there may well even be Sighs to help them take the hint.

Next comes the palaver of Getting Changed. Now if you're a practised beachgoer you may well have come prepared, with bathing gear already under your clothes. Then it's a just a matter of whipping off a T-shirt or a pair of shorts and you're ready. But often it's not that easy. It may be childish but I still find people's contortions as they try to change clothes in public enormously funny. There's the nonchalant "I'm just going to sit on the ground with a towel over my lap and hitch backwards and forwards" approach. At number two, there's the "I'm going to wrap this towel around me and wriggle around underneath it" style (with its variant in which the towel is held up by someone else who invariably drops it at an inopportune moment). Number one though is when you bring with you something that looks like a towelling marquee with a hole in it. You climb inside, stick your head through the hole and then fumble your way out of one set of clothes and into another - totally encased in fabric from neck to ankles. Your modesty will certainly be preserved, but the contortions do look like ferrets fighting in a sack.

This is the point at which I'm supposed to tell you all about my favourite beaches; the secret ones that not many people have discovered. The ones where there's never any litter on the tideline, where the sea's always warm, and where the sand is soft and white - the ones that the Famous Five scrambled down to between banks of honeysuckle and wild roses for picnics with lashings of ginger beer and thick ham sandwiches. Well, I'm not. Sorry. Apart from anything else *my* favourites may not turn out to be *your* favourites, and in any case what's the point of secret beaches if everyone else knows all about them? The fun is discovering them for yourself, after all. In any event I'm not sure that those "perfect" beaches actually do exist, so if you know of one then I'd keep it to yourself - after you've told me of course!

If you twisted my arm though, I would have to say that if you're in search of a beach that has just about something for everyone then you should head for Porthminster at St Ives. It's the one tucked under the railway station just on your right as you go into the town; in fact arriving by train is a fantastic way of getting there and certainly avoids all the hassle of trying to park a car in the town which always seems to be busy - even in winter. It must be one of the most impressive short train journeys in the country too. You can begin at either St Erth or the atmospherically named Lelant Saltings and then rattle along the coast (making sure you're sitting on the right hand side of the carriage for the best views) through the village, along to the mouth of the estuary and then over the dunes with glimpses of the coastline up towards Trevose Head. The track then runs through cuttings in the edge of the cliff amongst huge pine trees around Carbis Bay before you pull into St Ives station. If you have friends or relations visiting from up country I've found that this trip alone makes them green with envy as they suddenly realise that train journeys needn't always be overcrowded and delayed, with nothing to see through the grimy windows but litter-strewn sidings. From the station it's just a short stroll down a path to the sands. It's a beach that's cleaned regularly and where the crunchy sand is exactly the right texture for making sandcastles (if you've forgotten your bucket and spade there's even a little shop to sell you one). Looking to the left the greeny grey lichened rooftops of the town curve round to the island dotted with its little chapel and to the right you see the huge sweep of St Ives bay with Hayle and then Gwithian taking your eye away up the coast towards St Agnes beacon, Perranporth and beyond. From here you can see St Ives harbour too, and there's nothing better than sitting on the beach, looking up from your book from time to time, and being able to keep an eye on the comings and goings of the fishing boats, yachts and even the odd gig - the red of its hull vibrating against the blue of the sea.

And the sea here really is blue. The bluest blue there is. Really, really blue. For years artists have talked about the "quality of the light" in Penwith and if you come here you'll know exactly what they mean. Even in the winter the visibility is pin sharp; the shapes of each of the buildings stand out against one another and against the sky. It's not surprising then that the artist John Miller lives nearby.

For many years John lived in Sancreed, tucked away deep in the heart of the Penwith countryside, but an invitation to paint on Tresco in 1992, along with a move to the coast, opened up a completely new vision for him and now his paintings of the white sands, azure seas and the shades of blue of the skies above St Ives bay are recognised and hung in private collections and galleries all around the world. I even saw a John Miller print as part of the set on 'EastEnders'!

I first met John years ago when I went to interview him for a BBC Radio Cornwall documentary and I'm proud to say that we've been firm friends ever since. He's one of the most genuinely kind men I've ever known and has that rare ability to make everyone he speaks to feel as though they're the most interesting person he's ever met. Over the years John has also been an actor, a designer for the Rank organisation and an architect. He is now also a Lay Canon of Truro Cathedral and brings this wealth of experience to his paintings which, for me, are quite extraordinary and which, of course, do so much good for Cornwall. His book "Another Shade of Blue" explains that people as diverse as Toyah Willcox, Gary Rhodes and John le Carré are fellow fans and have visited his studio and caught a bit of "Miller magic" as well.

Back at my beach there are paintings too. These though are by Anthony Frost and are hanging on the blazing white walls of the Porthminster Beach Cafe. And it's the Cafe that makes Porthminster just about perfect for me. Forget a lukewarm thermos and sandy sandwiches. All you have to do is stagger a few yards from your towel or your deckchair for one of the best meals you'll ever eat in Cornwall. The Cafe's Head Chef is Cameron Jennings, an Australian who makes the most of locally caught seafood, and General Manager David Fox and the rest of the staff are unfailingly helpful and efficient. And what a view - once when I was there they even managed to lay on a dolphin cabaret! A school of about six of them leaped and jumped and generally showed off as they moved - with an accompanying flotilla of little boats - across the bay. Even without the dolphins, sitting on the cafe's terrace, the sunlight bouncing off the sand in front of you, looking at the brilliant sea and sky with a glass of wine and some freshly cooked fish you could be on some far-flung exotic holiday. But you're in Cornwall, which, of course, is even better.

At the end of the day the hill's shadow moves across the beach with sunbathers shifting across to make the most of the last rays until, at last, the sand begins to cool. For me this is almost the best part of the day. Many people have gone home by now and the sands are mostly empty but the air's still warm and you can see the sun glowing on the island across the harbour. Two or three gulls squabble over imaginary crumbs and sun-sore shoulders are eased gently back into T-shirts as you pack up and begin to head for home. Sandy feet squash into shoes. The next time they're worn they'll spill a reminder of the day. I guarantee it'll make you smile.

GWENNAP VILLAGE FETE
July

If the BBC had a penny for every time its presenters were asked to open a garden fete or chair a male voice choir concert then I reckon there'd be no need to raise the licence fee ever again. We all try to go along to as many as we can but sometimes things just aren't possible. On one Saturday in July I was already launching a new book about the West Cornwall painter Kurt Jackson in Newlyn in the evening and was going to a charity coffee morning in St Austell before lunch, so the day was quickly filled up when my old friend Catherine Mead asked me to open that afternoon's Gwennap Church Fete at her home, Pengreep House near Ponsanooth, mid way between Redruth and Falmouth.

Going along to a non-BBC event can be rather fraught. For a start because you work in radio and not TV, many people simply don't recognise you until you open your mouth. I remember a heated exchange in one of those huge DIY superstores when I was asking the bored couldn't-be-bothered-but-how-can-I-help-you cashier for a refund for a faulty electric drill. Almost losing my temper, I ranted on and on about how awful the drill was, how poor the shop's customer service was and why on earth didn't she just DO SOMETHING ABOUT IT!? Eventually giving in and handing me back my cash, she watched me sign the receipt. "Oh," she said, looking at my signature, "I thought it was you. I love the programme. I listen every day." I grabbed the cash and left the shop, shamefaced.

Other people aren't quite sure how to speak to you. On one hand you're a familiar name (and voice) to them but on the other you're someone who they don't physically recognise and who they don't actually know. It's like seeing a photograph of the actress who plays Shula Archer on BBC Radio 4; however you've imagined her in all those scenes at Brookfield Farm it's never like the picture you're looking at of Judy Bennett. "I thought you were older/younger/taller/shorter/thinner/fatter than that," people say to me and one lady famously came out with "Oh, I never heard that you had a beard!" as she asked for a signed photograph.

Being, apparently, such a familiar person does mean that total strangers seem to think that they can tell you all sorts of personal information as they would, maybe, members of their own family. I've lost track of how many surgical operations have been recalled in graphic detail, relations' misdemeanours revealed and family secrets laid bare - all in the space of a few minutes' chat!

So, when you do accept an invitation outside the safety of the studio you can seem to be taking your life in your hands. Some of the events you go to, of course, are superbly well run and everything goes smoothly. The organisers have asked you because they actually want *you*, and not because Jenny Agutter or Jean Shrimpton or one of the other celebrities who live in Cornwall were unavailable and, what's more, they spell your name correctly on the poster. They explain what they want you to do (and then don't change their minds!), they tell you what time you're expected, how long they want you to stay and where the lavatories are. It actually is as simple as that, so it's with great regret that I have to say that such well-run events are few and far between. Being introduced over the tannoy as "Tim Husband" doesn't fill you with confidence as to the success of the whole enterprise. Your heart sinks when someone says "and would you mind reading my daughter's story? There's only the ten chapters..." or "...And while you're here could you judge the baking competition?".

Now if there's one thing to guarantee making the ladies of a village hate you it's not to choose them as the first prize winner of a baking competition. Rivalry amongst the Victoria sponges can be fierce. Baby competitions are worse, of course, and after just one many years ago when, having not chosen her revolting child to win a cup, I was accosted by a very irate mother who shouted at me "Well, I bet you didn't look anything as a kid either!". I have firmly said no to judging them ever since. The problems don't stop there either. Fancy dress competitions can be minefields. Do you choose the little girl who looks immaculate as Snow White but whose entire outfit you know has been bought from the Disney Store or the 10 year old Darth Vader whose cardboard helmet and bits of tin foil aren't up to much but at least show some signs of effort and are home made?

Apart from judging events there's also the problem of The Stalls. As the Official Opener (even though the man at the gate didn't recognise you) it's the done thing to go around all the various stalls, comment on the weather, say nice things about how everyone's tried so hard this year and that, yes, the playing field/church roof/village hall/youth club is *such* a good cause, and make the odd purchase or two. The thing is that every stallholder expects your "one or two" purchases will come from them. By the end of the summer the freezer at home is stuffed with so many fete-bought fruit cakes and jam tarts that they see us through the whole winter and the plants I've bought could supply a whole series of "Gardeners' World". One or two of the stallholders I've met at village events could earn a fortune teaching the big supermarkets a thing or two about sales technique - you just can't walk away without buying something - anything! Embroidered tray cloths, stuffed toys, corn dollies, badly drawn sketches of St Michael's Mount (why are these at every fete I go to?), and wilting fuschia cuttings have all made their way into the boot of my car this year.

And then there's always The Raffle. I cannot bear raffles. I never win anything (well, I admit, a tin of Quality Street when I was at school) but I swear I wouldn't like them anyway. The raffle ticket seller is normally recruited from the upper ranks of the most successful high-pressure stallholder salespeople in previous fundraising campaigns. It takes a certain sort of nerve to walk up to total strangers and demand money and they have it. In spades. "Well they're 25p each," they say with a fixed smile. And then, just as you dig in your pocket for a 50p piece for two of them, they add quickly "or five for just £1!". Weakly you hand over a £1 coin. "It's much better value," they add brightly, "and of course you could win that lovely sketch of St Michael's Mount".

Then of course it's often you who has to draw the beastly thing. It's quite often at this point that the raffle organisers remember they haven't got a box or a barrel to put the ticket stubs in and, in my time, I've drawn winning numbers from old sacks, washing up bowls, supermarket carrier bags and even hastily emptied flower pots. You then have do battle with the crackly tannoy or just shout the numbers to a crowd of people who, by this stage in the afternoon, are busy packing up to go home.

"Yellow ticket, number 60!" you cry. No response.

"Yellow ticket, number 60!" you try again.

"Did he say 16?" a voice calls in the distance.

"I've got a blue ticket number 60," someone adds none too helpfully. Eventually it usually turns out that the local Vicar has the wining ticket and, as he is the person who's probably donated the sketch of St Michael's Mount in the first place, sportingly offers to forego his prize. I draw again. Nothing.

Now at this point each fete or concert organiser seems to have their own interpretation of the UK National Raffle Rules. Some maintain that an unclaimed ticket is re-drawn straight away. Some that the ticket holder will be contacted and

the prize duly delivered. At some fetes tickets of a certain colour go with certain types of prizes; pink - cakes, blue - plants and so on. Some say that certain prizes are allocated to the first, second and third tickets to be drawn, and others that each winner has a choice of the prizes that remain. This last option is inevitably a disaster, let me tell you. I still remember with squirming embarrassment a raffle I drew in the interval of a posh fashion show at Truro's old City Hall which went on for well over an hour. The models fumed backstage as the various winners firstly realised they'd won, then struggled out of their seats disturbing everyone else in

their row, made their way down to the stage and then spent ages agonising over whether they'd prefer the box of chocolates or, yes, the picture of the Mount, before returning to their seat, causing chaos in the audience all over again as I went on to read out the next winner's number. There were all of thirty prizes. Believe me, if you want to ruin the atmosphere of your concert/show/fete then this is one guaranteed way to do it.

Happily, back at Pengreep, a much jollier time was being had by all. When I arrived, a full half an hour before the two o'clock start, all sorts of stalls were up and running already - cakes and plants were doing a roaring trade, books and jumble showed nice promise and a coconut shy and home-made lemonade stand gave a nicely old fashioned touch. A glance into the huge kitchen revealed teams of ladies furiously jamming and creaming splits and scones for the teas and various other people were rushing about with rolls of sticky tape, marker pens and bags of loose change. Members of the Illogan Sparnon Silver Band in their super maroon uniforms began to gather in a semi-circle around the sundial in front of the house, the sun came out and all looked well.

Pengreep has a wonderful garden with a lake at the bottom of the lawns which slope away from the house. Visitors could be rowed around the lake, be taught how to fly fish, shoot a rifle or have a pony ride. What more could you ask for, and the crowds began to arrive in droves. There was a slight hiccup when the public address system failed at the last moment but with everyone's attention gathered by the simple expedient of Ben Mead bashing a metal dog's bowl with a handy screwdriver (such improvisation!) I said how nice it was to be there and declared the Gwennap Parish Church Fete well and truly open. I bought some cakes, had tea, declined the offer of a pony ride out of sympathy for the pony and listened to the band.

Then came time for the tug o' war - Pengreep House versus all comers. Now I'm quite used to having to turn my hand at pretty much anything at fetes like this, but I must admit I had never refereed a tug o' war before. The present holders of the Gwennap trophy - the team from the Lanner Inn - limbered up by knocking seven bells out of the coconut shy and then proclaimed themselves ready. I tried to look as if I knew what I was doing and watched as the marker on the rope moved first one way and then the other. After a few seconds it was obvious that the Lanner Inn team was going to wipe the floor with their opponents but they were generous enough to concede the first tug.

It didn't take long for bouts two and three to go to the Inn though and I ceremoniously handed back the wood and silver trophy to the pub's landlady so that it could be returned to its rightful place behind the bar. Justice had been seen to be done though and the children had fun with junior tug o' war for the rest of the afternoon until the thought of an ice cream proved just too strong and the rope lay abandoned on the lawn. Eventually, the crowds began to drift away and the tea makers, ice cream sellers and stallholders, hot and tired though they were, began to count their profits. All was well, one and all had enjoyed themselves and the Gwennap Church roof fund was almost a thousand pounds the richer.

FALMOUTH CLASSICS WEEK
August

"New yellow wellies and an ice bucket for the gin!" was what I was told I would need by one of my neighbours when I said that I was going along to Falmouth Classics; the yachties' annual get-together in Falmouth.

Now I knew that it wasn't exactly going to be all Blind Pew and "Fifteen men on the dead man's chest" but I hadn't realised that the general image of this sea and sail fest was quite so refined and quite so, well, snobbish. Mind you I still thought then that an Old Gaffer was a elderly man sitting on a park bench. I had a lot to learn.

Over the past few years Falmouth Classics has established itself as the opener to the Falmouth Regatta week - seven days of competition racing hosted by various local clubs. It's a weekend-and-a-bit full of receptions, racing, fireworks, concerts and a parade of sail with, as you'd imagine "classic" boats taking part from all over the United Kingdom. "But what is a classic boat?" was my first question and one I had to keep repeating because every time I asked it I got a different answer. "Any old thing with mahogany and a bit of brass" was the cynic's view, with other people trying to convince me of all sorts of strict technical criteria which they said allowed a boat to consider itself truly "classic". What did strike me was that everyone I spoke to who was involved in the Classics seemed to know one another, and then it dawned on me that the dozens of craft moored in the harbour and in the estuary - whatever else they had, or didn't have, in common - were part of one big floating homeless yacht club. Meeting up from time to time for Classics races in Paimpol in France or in Plymouth or in Fowey they all knew the cut of one another's jib. I also quickly gathered that while the participants might know one another, just like in any club, that didn't mean to say that everyone necessarily *liked* one another. Comments about missed marker buoys and poor seamanship were fired across the bows liked verbal cannonballs, but the numerous crates of beer and cases of wine being passed from deck to deck on the yachts rafted up alongside one another presumably made sure that things didn't go so far as anyone being made to actually walk the plank.

I'd been invited to go and watch the Parade of Sail from the water by friends who own an elderly wooden day boat, rather than my usual vantage point snug in the warm and dry sitting in the car eating an ice cream on Pendennis Head. *Watch* it, I should stress, as it's all taken very seriously and no real crew could afford to have someone like me - whose sailing experience amounts to a couple of day trips and once reading "Swallows and Amazons" - getting in the way. Two other friends, their two toddlers, a cousin, his grumpy teenage daughter and an excitable spaniel made up our crew and as we piled out of our cars and got together on the floating pontoons of Port Pendennis I had to admit we did look a motley bunch. Not even Captain Pugwash would have had us on board. A jumble of old sweatshirts, supermarket carriers spilling bread rolls and cartons of fruit juice, life-jackets, the dog's baskct ("it's the only way he'll keep still") and buckets and spades for the children (where did they think we were going?) certainly didn't compare with the neatly folded Guernsey sweaters, smart wicker picnic hampers and portable chilled drinks cabinets stowed on the gleaming cruiser moored alongside. Its occupants sat, chinking wine glasses in hand, looking down on us (in more ways than one) from their deck high above our heads.

We scrambled aboard, quietening the children but shouting at the dog and were just getting things shipshape and Bristol fashion, me hearties, when a sudden backwash of water hit us alongside. The children screamed, the dog barked, a bag of food fell into the harbour and we stumbled about in the tiny cockpit, grasping at each other like drunken dancers as we watched our neighbours roar away from their mooring and disappear out to sea. Perhaps there was something to be said for piracy after all. Eventually we too made our way out of the dock gate. What we lacked in style we made up for in enthusiasm as we briskly shouted commands (only some of which we understood) to one another. "Ready about!" "Lee Ho!" "Heel Away!" "Pass the beer!"

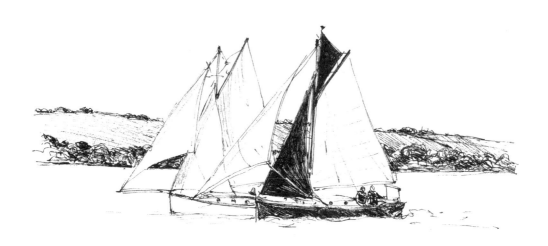

Many other people had had similar ideas and a little flotilla of assorted craft dotted the water, making their way from their moorings out into the bay. Looking back to Falmouth from the water you get to realise just how important the sea is to the town. With The Tower (what a place to live!) on the skyline, all the houses you see - many of them in terraces painted the pinks and greens and creams of Neapolitan ice cream - seem to jostle to get the best view. Their windows glinted in the sun, as did the dozens of pairs of binoculars trained on the gathering armada. The "Fraggle Rock" children's programmes made the St Anthony lighthouse into a bit of TV celebrity in its own right some years ago and our junior crew insisted we moored up within sight of it for our vantage point for the afternoon. The three youngest then set about trying to persuade the dog to jump off the boat into the water. ("Dogs can't drown, Daddy, God won't let them. I read it on the Internet," - a convincing argument if ever I heard one.) Grumpy teenager ("Where's the sun cream? A tan is so un-cool.") retreated into the cabin with a Walkman and a stack of CDs, and the rest of us found bits of deck of varying degrees of comfort on which to sit and tried to look as though we knew our stem from our stern.

The whole expedition could have been a disaster but the Classics' Parade of Sail was wonderful (and no mistake, Jim lad). From where we were parked, sorry, moored, just off Trefusis Headland the winners and losers alike sailed past us. Tan sails smacking in the wind, fluttering flags, gleaming brass, polished wood - this was the chance for everyone to show off their boats at their best and they took it. The bay was filled with sail as before our eyes they tacked and gibed and came about to order like dressage horses flaunting themselves in front of the judges. Of course they had a huge tradition to live up to. Years ago the saying "Falmouth for Orders" used to be heard around the world and in the eighteenth and nineteenth centuries clippers, schooners and the local pilot cutters would have made a similar spectacle. By the end of the afternoon, as the Parade dispersed and with no more than a tot of rum from the captain's secret stash under the deck boards, it was easy to imagine the town in its sailing hey day. We started for home. There, surely, under Pendennis Headland, was the Hispaniola.

SITTING IN THE SUN AT MINIONS
August

You know it's amazing what fund raisers ask you to do in the name of the BBC. In my time I've been "rescued" from the sea by the Search and Rescue helicopter from RNAS Culdrose and been sponsored to race around all of the Isles of Scilly for Children in Need. I've even come down to earth with rather more than a bump in a hot air balloon, when a sudden squall of wind dragged us bouncing across two fields before we finally came to rest upside down - and certainly worse for wear - in a thorn hedge! So I was on the lookout for, shall we say, a quieter way of raising some cash for charity, when an invitation landed on my desk. It was to play a Cornish version of boules for a BBC Radio Cornwall team in one of my favourite Bodmin Moor villages and I accepted straight away. The only thing was, first I had to get there. Minions is some fifty miles from where I live - fifty miles of the A30 crammed with August Saturday morning holiday traffic.

The queues proved every bit as bad as I had thought. Over the years I have interviewed dozens of people about the proposed dualling of the stretch of single carriageway that runs across the Goss Moor in-between Indian Queens and Bodmin. Businessmen tell me that if Cornwall is to have an effective communications system then it's vital that the road is widened. Environmentalists say that any road works would destroy valuable heathland and councillors claim that they have no money and that they need government grants to eke out their transport budgets. Now, don't get me wrong, I love Cornwall's countryside as much as anyone, and I know that our health service and schools deserve as much cash as they can get, but as I sat for an hour or so in a huge queue of overheating cars filled with impatient holidaymakers and their fractious children I must confess I began to think that losing a few yards of gorse bushes and spending a few quid on some tarmac maybe wasn't such a bad idea.

By the time I had driven through the Glynn Valley the traffic had thinned out a bit and as I left the A38 and rattled over the cattle grid onto Bodmin Moor things seemed decidedly better. I always enjoy going to Minions, which is a lovely village with granite houses, a couple of shops and a pub all tucked into any bit of shelter they can find. You can understand why because the winds up here are fierce and must blow from September right through to August. The views are spectacular in every direction with old and new Cornwall - on one hand the Caradon Hill TV and radio transmitter mast and on the other the Cheesewring and the Hurlers stones - proving equal attractions for visitors.

A quick glance at some of the other teams told me that Michael Taylor, my fellow BBC Radio Cornwall team mate, and I might have been better just to have put a cheque in the post. We were entering for fun and to raise a bit of cash but lots of other people seemed to be taking the whole thing very seriously. Several people were striding confidently around the pitches who'd obviously played the game before (which was one up on us for a start). They wore matching "sports casual" outfits, proper shoes and seemed to know the difference between an "end", a "round" and a "match" and the most professional looking of them even had little magnets on bits of cord wound around like yo-yos to retrieve their balls and looked on smugly as the rest of us groped around in the wet grass and the sheep muck.

I was still looking forward to an afternoon pottering around in the sunshine but no sooner had we started than we were knocked out in the first round! It was definitely a game of one half, Brian, and that was that. The tournament was due to last for most of the day and it was still only eleven o'clock in the morning so, trying not to look unduly upset by my defeat, I walked across the road to the Minions Post Office and Shop which is run by Nigel and Lisa Drew. Stone and slate hung, and with its St Piran's flag hanging outside, it seems to me that it's just about everything a village shop should be. It's even got a blackboard outside on which is written the day's weather forecast and tethering posts for both dogs AND horses! A sign proclaims it to be "the highest Post Office in Cornwall" and another that they are "open most hours for most things" next to a old fashioned wheeled barrow piled high with fresh fruit and veg. Inside they've got a tearoom, a small off-licence and the Post Office as well as just about anything you could ever need. What more could you want? Oh, yes, a mid morning cup of coffee and a biscuit - and they do that too. On a tray. Outside on a bench in the sun. Lovely.

Minions has another claim to fame, of course. It's around here that many of the sightings of the so-called "Beast of Bodmin Moor" are made, and Nigel Drew has started a register in his shop to log these events as and when they happen. He showed me the entries, which all seemed to record remarkably similar details and, he assured me, were made by remarkably sensible people. Muddy, beigey, fawn coloured or black. Muscular or lean. Big cats - the size of large alsatians. Noticeably long tails. Over the years of course, in other parts of Cornwall, there has been other evidence - the odd bit of fuzzy video, plaster casts of some large paw prints, the remains of savaged sheep and two remarkable photographs which appeared on the front of the local "Cornish Guardian" in 1998 taken on a rocky cliff path. I've spoken several times to former moorland farmer Rosemary Rhodes who lives near Ninestones. She tells me that she's seen several cats over the years and that a black "beast" took up residence near the farm one season and was frequently seen with her cub playing alongside. Rosemary's seen fawn coloured pumas too and she's also had reported sightings in nearby woods of a lynx with its characteristically pointed ears and bob tail.

Each batch of sightings of course leads to fresh speculation and experts claiming that the only proof that they can accept of cats living in the wild in Cornwall would be a carcass or a skeleton. How sad that would be. I have spoken to sufficient people whose accounts are so convincing that, even though I have seen nothing myself, I firmly believe that there are groups of cats living wild. But I have to say I am happy not to know. These days too many ideas and issues are seen in simplistic black and white. Scientists and technology between them have explained away many of the mysteries surrounding our lives and too often I hear the phrase "the secret can be revealed". Well, I'm quite happy for there to be a few secrets kept, thank you very much, and for one or two mysteries to remain. The shades of grey have a lot going for them in my book.

As the tournament went on (and on) I sat on the stone wall outside the pub and looked across the miles and miles of moor stretching away in front of me. You hear a lot of people say that the coastline provides the best scenery in Cornwall but, for my money, those big cats have got some of the best views going - let's hope they don't find *us* too beastly and stay around to enjoy them.

THE NEWLYN FISH FESTIVAL
August

If you want to hear a good tale - tall or not - then a harbour is the place to be. Fishermen, fishes and fishing are the very stuff of stories, legends, dreams and, sadly, nightmares. From the memories of "the one that got away", through a wealth of Christian symbolism to fabled monsters living in the deep, the relationship between fish and men has always been just that bit special.

Every year the Newlyn Fish Festival sets out to celebrate that relationship and to raise cash for the Fishermen's Mission into the bargain. Not too many people realise that Newlyn is one of the largest ports in the UK and regularly handles about £22,000,000 of landings each year - some 12,000 tonnes of fish. A few days before the Festival I got up very early in the morning to see the market in action. The yellow of the men's oilskins stood out in the mist still hanging over the water, their colour made even more vivid by the bright fluorescent light inside the new shed. The men's voices (for this is, by and large, men only territory) bounced off the concrete walls and fish boxes slithered along the ground in a whoosh of crushed ice, pushed from one man to another as if they were playing a very strange giant board game. They obviously understood the rules - and the language and procedures of the auction bidding - but I really hadn't a clue what was going on.

I felt completely outside the whole thing. It was like a very exclusive club and I was not a member. Everyone was friendly enough and there was a lot of good-humoured banter flying around but this was not a place for strangers. Looking around the sheds - even at that time in the morning - many of the boxes were already labelled with French or Spanish buyers' names. Harbour Master Andrew Munson, who was good enough to show me round, told me that most of the fish landed in the port goes direct to the continent and never sees a British kitchen.

The market also has to cope with the fickle tastes of the public. For some reason which I can't understand, housewives (and househusbands I suppose, for let's not be sexist about this) don't seem to be able to cope with the idea of buying a fish *au naturel* and preparing it at home, yet they seem quite happy to haul giblets out of supermarket chickens. Horror stories of members of the Royal Family and fish bones stuck in throats do the rounds and yet the people who recount them with a shudder think nothing of "mechanically recovered" meat (just don't ask!) in various processed pies and pasties.

I'm told that there are various fish marketing boards and I feel sorry for all of them. One of the other problems they have to cope with is how certain species of fish can move in and out of fashion. The odd word of praise on TV by a celebrity chef or an unfavourable comment by a diet guru in the Sunday supplements can cause shock waves to ripple through the market which have more effect than those pounding the harbour wall. In years gone by fish such as gurnard, coley, or even not that long ago monkfish, would have been used for bait or for feeding the cat. Now they're to be found on the best restaurant tables - overseas and at home.

The industry, of course, is one of the most dangerous in the world and, sadly, I present radio reports of tragedies at sea all too often. The official figures tell me that every month around the UK ten men are either killed or seriously injured at sea, but the statistics can't begin to describe the personal tragedies that they represent. Recently though there seems to have been some real progress in improving sea safety. There have been more and more calls for the government to approve a design of lifejacket which doesn't get in the way on board a working boat, EPIRB distress signal systems have been introduced and, in Newlyn itself, a coded system of "reporting in" called the FRS (the Fishermen's Reporting System) is becoming more popular. Of course a death at sea can be doubly tragic as it often means that there is not even a funeral or an opportunity for a last goodbye.

Superintendent David Mann from the Newlyn Fishermen's Mission tells me that, no matter how often he has to do it, breaking the news of men missing at sea to their families is always a difficult and traumatic one, knowing that, as he knocks on the door, the lives of the family will never be the same again after his visit. Perhaps we'd all do well when we look at the cost of a piece of cod or plaice in the supermarket to remember the true price of fish.

This year's Festival - the ninth - on the August Bank Holiday weekend was one of the busiest ever. Having been there before I abandoned any attempt to park nearby and took advantage of the free bus that crawled through the crowds backwards and forwards from Penzance railway station. Travelling to Newlyn along the seafront I shared the journey with a family from Manchester who were in Cornwall on holiday. They seemed to have got the idea that the Festival was some sort of ancient Celtic ceremony - all in the Cornish language - in praise of fish, and asked me if I thought they'd be able to understand what was going on. I had a picture in my mind of Monty Python's fish-slapping dance routine but was just beginning to explain the truth when we arrived at Newlyn harbour. I am ashamed to say I left them to discover what was actually going on for themselves and spent the rest of the day trying to avoid them!

Everyone else seemed to know exactly why they were there though and took the opportunity to explore the ice plants, the trade stands, the cookery demonstrations and to walk along the piers with an ice cream taking a look at the boats, flags flying in the wind. British International Helicopters put in an appearance for a guess-the-height-of-the helicopter competition (well it made a change from guessing the weight of a cake), and at half past four the fish market held an auction. The quantities were rather smaller than usual - kilos instead of tonnes - but the bidding was just as strong and the humour just as liberal as I'd seen early in the morning a few days before. Plastic carrier bags bulged and ballooned on the floor of the bus and recipe leaflets were stuffed into pockets as we headed back to Penzance. We all knew what we'd be having for supper tonight.

WALKING 'COAST TO COAST'
August

One of Cornwall's pride and joys is the coastal footpath and one of my pride and joys is that, after more than twenty years of living in Cornwall, I've managed to walk most of it. Not all together, you understand, just in little bits and pieces, most of which can be done in less than a day and most of which involve an hour or so in a pub or a tea shop.

Years before I joined the BBC I used to listen in the mornings to BBC South West on Radio Four when producers Guy Slatter and Chris Blount (both of whom I was later to have the pleasure of working with at BBC Radio Cornwall) and the wonderful Bill Best Harris made a series of programmes as they walked the South-west's entire stretch along both North and South coasts to Land's End, accompanied by Bill's labrador Honey.

Hearing them describe the sights they saw, and talk to the characters they met along the way, made me think that, one day, I would try to follow in their boot steps. Cornwall can claim over 600 kilometres of the path, which twists and turns and drops and climbs over some of the most spectacular coastal scenery - let's not be modest about this - in the world. The variety in the landscape is just enormous - the miles of sand dunes at Perranporth, the deserted mining landscapes of Cape Cornwall, the wooded estuaries of the Fal and the Helford, and, in Penwith, the spectacularly weathered granite cliffs at Nanjizal and Pednevounder.

I'm often asked which is the stretch of the coast I enjoy the most and it's a question I find virtually impossible to answer. There are so many. It depends of the weather and the tide, the season and the time of day. Somewhere in my "top ten" would have to be a walk from the picturesque Penberth Cove eastwards past the tiny flower meadows towards Mousehole. St Ives to Zennor is a favourite stretch as is The Kelseys, the headland south of Crantock beach and Polly Joke. Port Quin to Polzeath on the North Coast has to be in the list too and, on the South coast, around Polruan and Fowey and on the Roseland. Having been used to doing much of my walking west to east or east to west I jumped at the chance of walking south to north and literally "coast to coast". It was suggested that, taking the title of the walk from the BBC Radio Cornwall programme "Coast to Coast" which I present, listeners should be invited to come along and, if they wished, organise sponsorship for themselves to help a Cornish charity.

Bank Holiday Monday was decided upon as a date when many people would be free and when, hopefully, the weather would be kind. The Mineral Tramways Project, based at Old Cowlin's Mill at Carn Brea near Redruth, has been responsible for developing several walks in the area, for example along the Great Flat Lode and the Tresavean Trail near Lanner and Jane Buchanan, Marketing Coordinator from the Project, very kindly volunteered to help us out. We really had no idea how many people would take up the challenge we had set and at the last minute I had visions of just Jane and me plodding quietly along in the rain on our own. I certainly couldn't have hoped for better walking weather - sunny, but not too warm and with a good breeze and I couldn't have hoped for a better welcome as I arrived at our starting point at Perranwell Station to be greeted by nearly two hundred listeners and Radio Cornwall staff, along with assorted children and (very) assorted dogs!

Now, before you ask, yes, I know that Perranwell Station isn't actually on the coast but for safety's sake Jane had wisely decided that we should all get together where there was room to meet, for people to be dropped off and to park cars. As soon as we had started the line of walkers began to spread out, and as we headed down into the valley we crossed the Carnon River just as it becomes Restronguet Creek so you see it *was* the coast. Well, sort of! Those in front set a good pace and soon we had passed the former Point Mills Arsenic Refinery and the Nangiles Adit. I discovered that the workers there had to have specially made wooden nails in their boots as metal ones rusted too quickly because the ground was so contaminated by chemicals. It seemed strange to think that the countryside through which we were walking - complete with water lilies and dragon flies - had once been such a polluted and industrial landscape. Photographs were taken, some sketches made and we walked on. Chatting to fellow walkers along the route I was amazed to hear their tales. Quite elderly people put me to shame with their stories of dozens of miles walked in one day in the middle of winter and genteel ladies who looked as though they'd be more at home pruning roses told me how they regularly scythed and macheted their way through briars and gorse to keep their favourite paths open.

The Mineral Tramways Project is working to upgrade the "Coast to Coast" trail so that all of it is suitable for horse riders and cyclists as well as walkers. These days I quite often see entire families out cycling and it must be that there are almost as many cyclists around nowadays as there were in the old push bike's hey day of the 1950s, although modern technology means that their multi-speed, lightweight descendants have little in common with their sit-up-and-beg forebears. Health reasons (either their own or the planet's) are pushing people into pushing pedals and it's good to see that they're being encouraged by cycle ways alongside main roads and what's becoming a huge network of cycle routes all over the UK.

Back on two feet, by lunchtime some people (well, me actually) were beginning to flag but lunch in a Scorrier pub revived spirits and we set off again, now heading for Portreath along the Old Tramroad. This was the first surfaced tramroad in Cornwall and was built so that horses could haul wagons of ore from the inland mines to the harbour, and then Welsh coal to fuel those same mine engines back in the other direction. Although it was never a passenger line the directors of the company which owned it had their own special carriage in which to ride (which you can still see in the Royal Cornwall Museum) and by this stage in the afternoon one or two people had begun to wish that they too were being carried towards their destination.

Portreath was now in sight, and though these days the harbour has been infilled with boxy brick modern houses and amusement arcades edge its beachside car park, it still shows the signs of once being one of the county's most important ports. I wondered what Laurence Binyon thought of the place when he wrote the famous

> At *the going down of the sun and in the morning*
> *We will remember them*

in 1914 up on the cliffside at the "Pepperpot" Daymark.

Thankfully the final section of the route was relatively easy, dropping down the hillside, along the route of the famous Portreath Incline railway - the "marvel of the age" which was eventually to replace the Tramway. Eventually we got to the harbourside to cross a finishing line, have well earned cup of tea, and be rewarded with a certificate to prove that everyone really had walked "Coast to Coast".

SURFERS AGAINST SEWAGE BALL
September

I have to come clean, if you'll pardon the pun, and say that the first time I went to a Surfers Against Sewage Ball I was rather apprehensive. Would my interpretation of the "black tie and board shorts" dress code be correct? Would the rave music be too loud? And more than anything wouldn't I be, well, just too *old*? I needn't have worried.

This annual ball, a party held for SAS members and their guests on the first Friday of September each year, is quite the most extraordinary event I've come across in Cornwall. Take three thousand ecologically aware outrageously dressed party-animals, put them into Cornwall's largest sequence of marquees on the edge of a cliff on the north coast, turn up the volume of the live music, add food and drink and stand well back!

I'm told that the first ball was, by today's standards, a relatively low key affair but, since 1990, the event has grown to such an extent that people fly in to Newquay airport from all over the world just to be seen there. Of course the growth in the popularity of the ball has gone along with the rise of Surfers Against Sewage as an environmental campaigning organisation. Its founder, Chris Hines, tells me that he never imagined at the start of the campaign that he would have become a national spokesman on pollution issues - called upon almost daily by newspapers, television and radio stations for a comment or a quote.

It may be unfortunate that the name Surfers Against Sewage means that many people who wouldn't know "Blue Juice" from orange juice feel that the message is not for them. In Cornwall we live our lives surrounded on three sides by the ocean and surely it's important to all of us that not only the quality of that sea water is as good as it possibly can be, but that our beaches are as clean as possible too. I'm sure that everyone has their own horror story of some sort of revolting rubbish that they've come across. Years ago, beachcombing was a real pleasure. You'd stroll along the tideline (with bare feet of course) turning over shells, driftwood and other "treasures" - nowadays it can be more like a walk across a garbage tip.

It's hard to underestimate the importance of the coastline to visitors to Cornwall as well and from time to time I wonder what sort of impression some of our most polluted beaches must give when holiday stories are swapped and photographs pored over in homes in the Midlands or in London. As a campaigning organisation the group's certainly had its work cut out but there is good news. When SAS began, single-screened long sea outfalls were the norm but changes have been made and regulations have been tightened up. Nowadays more and more ultra-violet disinfection is taking place and the sea is definitely a cleaner - and safer - place, although the group's efforts certainly aren't letting up and it now has set its sights on European as well as British waters.

Tonight, though, was for celebrating what's been achieved rather than worrying about the future. This year's theme was Glo Ball ("global" - clever, eh?) and in the days beforehand I can tell you that there wasn't a drop of fluorescent paint to be had in Cornwall for love nor money. I have never seen such extraordinary costumes; everyone was glowing in one form or another. Illuminated hats, sparkling wands, shimmering ball gowns or luminous face paint seemed to be the order of the day. Stilt walkers danced alongside hordes of Austin Powers lookalikes and Ziegfeld showgirls with beads, rhinestones and feather headdresses paraded through the crowds. Some days before a Great White had apparently been seen off the north coast near Port Isaac and this meant that several shark outfits put in an appearance and the environmental theme was kept up by two people dressed together as the Exxon Valdez oil tanker.

The line-up of the bands appearing at the ball is always kept secret but, since I've been going anyway, this hasn't stopped wild rumours flying around the St Agnes area about which stars are, or are not, apparently going to be making an appearance. The Rolling Stones, Oasis and U2 have all been mentioned and Katy Barnes, from SAS, tells me that she even once heard that Madonna would be performing. Even this year I was very confidently told by a girl wearing glowing devil's horns, phosphorescent paint and very little else that "Boy George is in the VIP area...he wants to support SAS.". Well, George may well want to support SAS I don't know, but I can tell you that he certainly wasn't there when I sneaked in around the tent flap. I have to confess I was relieved to find the volume of the bands on stage was slightly quieter in here and was also pleased to find some (suitably glowing) air filled sofas and chairs. As I sat down I exchanged apologetic and embarrassed glances with some of the other people who also seemed to be finding the going a bit tough in the main marquee and we mumbled remarks about "at my age", "just for a minute," and "my back".

Republica were the headline act this year and their lead singer Saffron said that she thought the Ball was such a lovely event to play at "because the people are so nice". And they are. In the years I've been going there and with the thousands and thousands of people who've been there with me I've never even heard of an argument and the atmosphere's always been welcoming and friendly. I may feel my age, and I might find the music just a tad too loud but I've already got my costume planned for next year and, though I'm not one to spread rumours, I'm looking forward to meeting Boy George.

LANTERN-MAKING WORKSHOP
October

If, like me, you've admired at those huge glowing paper lanterns with ribs of willow which you see carried at events such as Truro's Christmas City of Lights or Mousehole's Tom Bawcock's Eve celebrations, you wouldn't have turned it down either. My friend Keri Jessiman from Falmouth's Miracle Theatre was on the 'phone asking if I wanted to go to a lantern-making workshop. She was thinking of booking a place and did I want to go too?

Ten days later we were driving along some of the tiniest and prettiest lanes I've yet to come across, somewhere between Gweek and Helston, like two eager children, excited but a bit nervous, off for their first day at school. What would our teacher be like, had we remembered our dinner money and would we have something to bring home to show our Mums? We were heading for Tresahor Vean, a lovely granite house a good way off the lane down a bumpy track, with a series of barn workshops and studios on the opposite side of its courtyard.

Jenny and Pete Leighton host a year round programme of events, workshops and classes attracting people from all over the county - and beyond - who come to try their hand at things like print making, sculpture, paper making or casting. Teacher for the day was Tessa Garland who also makes these lanterns professionally. Some of them decorated the Tresahor Vean studio - huge willow-and-white tissue floor lamps glowed ethereally, while sophisticated bronzed wire table lights and shades overlaid with pierced metal were reminders of the standard we were aiming for.

About a dozen of us met over a welcoming cup of coffee and hung around a warming woodburning stove as Tessa unloaded boxfuls of tools, cutting boards, glue, reels of copper wire, bundles of withies, soldering irons and reams of pristine white tissue paper. I could see that this was going to be a playgroup for grown ups - a "Blue Peter" effort of the most sophisticated kind. I tried to put Joyce Grenfell's gently mocking monologue about WI members making "useful and acceptable gifts from hazelnut clusters" out of my mind as I looked again at some of the lanterns Tessa had made from copper wire rather than willow. Seeing coils and coils of it gleaming enticingly in loops around the floor both Keri and I quickly abandoned

our thoughts of making something Big and Willowy for something Small and Wiry instead.

Everyone was rather nervous about starting - putting the first bend or twist in the wire was like writing the first word on a page or putting the first brushful of paint on a piece of canvas - but, once we had started, we were away. Within a few minutes the room was a sea of people wrestling with lengths of wire, like firemen struggling with water filled snaking hosepipes, trying to make them do in practice what they could see in their mind's eye. Hammers, pliers and saws were wielded and it wasn't long before the gas torches were lit and the smell of solder (and, it has to be said, charred wood from a couple of the tables) was in the air. Gradually, out of nothing, wire frames appeared - circular, spiral, square, hexagonal.

The sense of achievement was obvious as we all began to realise that we were actually creating something for ourselves. Compliments were offered, and accepted, across the room and it made me realise that it really was a playgroup for grown ups and how rarely most of us get the chance to do something creative. Even if you accept that only a few people can earn a living as a potter, a painter or a poet, it's amazing to think of the amount of creative opportunities we deny ourselves; we buy a ready meal rather than cook with raw ingredients and we go for a "low maintenance" garden rather than one we actually have to work in. Of course there are often good reasons why we make those choices but it seems to me that somewhere along the line we're missing out.

Back at Tresahor it was time for a break. It turned out that there were no measly school dinners for us but a superb home cooked lunch (with two puddings!) was brought across the courtyard, along with the chance to chat to other people. A couple of mums having a Saturday to themselves, a solicitor, a gym teacher and a landscape gardener all swapped stories and welding hints, compared wire shapes and solder blisters and then off we went again. Now the frames were becoming more and more flamboyant; legs, brackets, and elaborate curlicues were soldered one on top of the other until Tessa called a halt - The Papering had to begin.

This was the messy bit. Basically we mixed washing up bowls full of very runny glue and then tried to drape soaked pieces of tissue paper across our frames. Soggy lumps of paper splattered down on to the tables but by now our blood was up, the clock was ticking toward Home Time, and we would not be put off. Like a slapstick scene from a pantomime, glue was furiously pasted on to paper (and anything else that got in the way) and layer after layer found itself wrapped around what were now - almost recognisably - lamps.

We stood back and surveyed our efforts. Keri had a neat, box-shaped table job with curly wire legs. I had a (sort of) wall lamp with blobby wire decorations at the top (none at the bottom, mind you, as I'd confused centimetres and inches and run out of wire!) and the lady with whom I'd shared several moments of welding despair over a gas flame now had a masterpiece that was nothing short of a chandelier! Tessa said that we'd all done Jolly Well Indeed and we all wondered who she thought was top of the class.

As we cleared up and began to load our precious (but still dripping) lamps into car boots and drive away home into the autumn evening, it was as if we were all leaving primary school at the end of the Christmas term with our calendars and advent crowns. Whatever we'd made and whatever it looked like we knew our mums would be proud of us and to them *we* were the ones with the gold stars whatever anyone else may say.

POSTSCRIPT

Now finished (although it took weeks to dry hanging on a radiator and so added pounds to the electricity bill) and coloured with Indian inks, my humble effort is hanging on the conservatory wall.

"That's an, er, interesting lamp," visitors say. "Where did you buy it?" Now it turns out that all that wire and welding, and all that paper and ink I sloshed on, don't actually allow much light from the bulb to shine through. Some - unkind - people might call it a design fault but at least it means they can't see me grinning.

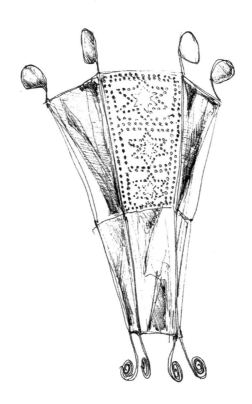

A WOODLAND DAY AT TRELISSICK GARDEN
November

Trelissick Garden near Truro has to be just about my favourite National Trust property in Cornwall. Yes, I know that Lanhydrock House is a finer building, that Mount Edgcumbe, Glendurgan and Trengwainton all boast wonderful gardens and that Trerice is a near perfect example of a manor house and garden of its day. For me, though, Trelissick is just about as good an example as you're going to get of what the Trust is all about, as it rolls its message of stewardship and conservation into the new millennium. There's the parkland for a start. Acres and acres of rolling pasture and woodland with, on one side, huge skies and sweeping views right across Falmouth Bay over to the Lizard and, on the other, more intimate glimpses between the oaks which lean down to touch the water of the quiet and reflective Lamouth Creek. You ask a local dog if they know of anywhere better for their owner to exercise them and they'll agree with me I'm sure.

At the centre of the estate the usual National Trust shop and National Trust tea room (it tastes all the better for being served by a nice smiley lady in a floral pinny, you know) sit alongside a restaurant housed in a magnificent former barn. On top of that a unique partnership between the Cornwall Crafts Association and the Trust means that a former store is now a first rate gallery with paintings and craft of the highest quality from all over the county.

Of course most people come for the garden itself and undoubtedly it's everything a Cornish garden should be. There are wild bits, colourful bits and woody bits, waterside bits, formal bits and flowery bits. There's even a long semi-tropical bit in the valley alongside the road running down to the King Harry Ferry - all in the care of Head Gardener, and supporter of all things Cornish, Barry Champion. Many people would say the garden's at its best in the spring (along with many others in the county) but I can find something new just about whenever I visit. The Queen Mum, on a private visit to Cornwall a few years ago, trundled around in her electric buggy quite merrily in the middle of the summer and seemed very happy so I think I'm in good company.

But it's the extras (what these days seems to be called "added value" in the same way that the perfectly acceptable words "way of life" have been replaced by the ghastly "lifestyle" and "given the job" by the excruciating "tasked") that the property offers which makes it so special for me and for the hundreds of thousands of visitors who go there every year. Theatre or music performances in the grounds, exhibitions in the courtyard, schools workshops, nature trails, garden tours, carol singing, craft demonstrations and beachcombing searches, not forgetting Father Christmas in the stables, all attract both locals and holidaymakers and of course bring in all-important income.

So, there I was on a sunny Saturday in November, avoiding the cowpats and tramping across the fields towards a thicket of trees from which thin columns of blue grey smoke were spiralling skywards. This was Trelissick's "Woodland Day" organised by Area Warden Neil Stephenson. Surprisingly for the time of year the

day was dry and bright and, once inside, I had to adjust my eyes to the relative shade of the copse. What emerged from the gloom was almost like Robin Hood's camp in Sherwood Forest. Showers of woodchips flew away from a foot powered lathe, hazel sticks were being shaped into chairs and two charcoal burner ovens were gently smoking and scenting the air. It was that unmistakable autumnal bonfire smell which hovers between leafmould and damp dog. All that was needed was Friar Tuck stirring a huge cauldron of venison stew (Restaurant Manager please take note for next time). It really was as if the tiny wood had become a time capsule, for two working horses which had been moving enormous tree trunks just as they would have done on the estate a hundred years ago, stood now amongst the trees sweating and stamping and shaking their harness.

And people loved it. Enthusiastic dogwalking couples in matching waxed jackets and hiking boots diverted from the footpath to watch the woodturner and an elderly lady in tweeds was peering over her specs and intently quizzing the charcoal burner about the quality of his finished product. Hordes of children had to be enticed from gazing at the skills of the adze-wielding woodcraftsman and of Graham Brown from nearby Cowlands Creek who was weaving traditional willow baskets. So, lots of people through the gates; a great success.

But of course quite often it's not as simple as that. It strikes me that the National Trust has got a very difficult job on its hands. In these days of "access" and "accountability" its growing membership is demanding a greater say in what goes on and increasingly greater facilities at the properties. More people, though, means more wear and tear - not just inside the houses but on garden lawns, cliff paths and beaches. Then, when the Trust tries to limit the damage such numbers cause, by restricting opening hours, paving access paths or restoring a derelict outhouse to become an extra loo, they're accused of "manicuring" and "gentrifying". It seems they just can't win.

Where the National Trust *has* won, and won spectacularly, is in protecting hundreds of miles of Cornish coastline from commercial development. The national policy of buying "one farm back" from the cliff edge (which actually started in Cornwall) has meant that the entire coastal landscape up to the first skyline is saved rather than just a narrow strip of land along the shore. As recently as the 1930s a huge amount of the coastline near Trelissick - from Turnaware Point to St Mawes - was threatened with a massive docks development. Now the Trust owns much of the land around Carrick Roads and, in fact, about 40% of the Cornish coast.

Last year I showed two friends from Australia around Cornwall. They said their favourite day was one spent on Pendower Beach ("the one with the green oak leaf sign") and couldn't quite believe it when I told them it was owned and looked after by a charity rather than the government. "You should be so proud of it," they said. I told them that we were.

TRURO'S CITY OF LIGHTS
December

I am not a shopper. I am particularly not a late night Christmas shopper. The thought of fighting my way through hordes of people wandering about - usually in the cold and the pouring rain - trying to choose between buying Dad the tie in Marks and Spencer or the socks in Littlewoods fills my troubled mind with very mighty dread indeed. Over the years I've devised a simple four point guide to Christmas shopping.

1. Decide what you want.   2. Go into a shop.   3. Buy it.   4. Go home.

Simple, isn't it. So why doesn't everyone do it? Each year shopkeepers try to kid us that by playing endless tapes of "Rudolph The Red Nosed Reindeer" or "Jingle Bells" and by draping a bit of tinsel across their displays, shopping at Christmas somehow becomes enjoyable. I, for one, refuse to believe it.

Buying presents for children is the worst of all. Each year there seems to be one particular toy that, apparently, they *must* have. Years ago this might have been something as simple as a hoop and top but now it's likely to be either some sort of bizarre cuddly toy with big eyes peering from a bundle of fake fur or a computer game in which aliens are violently annihilated in a crescendo of explosions and flashing lights.

A couple of years ago you may remember the craze was for Teletubbies. These strange plump creatures with TV sets in their stomachs had become all the rage after the BBC featured them in a series for pre-school children. They were picky with their food and ate nothing but toast and custard, rolled around on the grass a lot and spoke vaguely unintelligible English. A bit like children themselves really. Predictably anyone under five loved them and anyone over fifty hated them but, that year, *they* were the toy to have. The problem was that they were so popular they were in very short supply. I had been very sceptical about all the Teletubby hype but, in a rash moment, had volunteered to buy a model of one of the characters for a friend's daughter. I should have known better. As I couldn't quite bring myself to say "Excuse me, have you got a La La?" to total strangers over the telephone, I was forced to abandon my own four point shopping plan and actually traipse from shop to shop with everyone else trying to track one of the beastly things down. You would never have believed that this was the season of goodwill if you'd witnessed the temper tantrums, tears and foot stamping that I saw that afternoon. And that was just the adults.

So, all in all, I was not entirely filled with Christmas cheer when I was asked to put in an appearance at the BBC Radio Cornwall stall - set up in Boscawen Street with dozens of others - on the first of Truro's late night shopping evenings. Little did I know I was to be in for a treat. This particular night was also the date of the fourth of Truro's City of Lights festivals. The event gets its name from the illuminated lanterns - made from willow withies and paper - which are then paraded in musical processions.

There's a wonderful painting in the Royal Cornwall Museum called "Jubilee Celebrations in a Cornish Village" which shows a children's procession illuminated by Chinese lanterns and Tony Crosby, one of the organisers and founding artists of

the City of Lights project, tells me that there has always been a strong tradition of lantern parades in Cornwall. Alice King and Anna Murphy from Kneehigh Theatre had great success with lantern parades in Mousehole to celebrate Tom Bawcock's Eve a few years ago and in 1996 it was decided to extend the idea to Truro with a procession of lanterns based on the buildings of the city. Since then the whole thing has grown enormously so that this year eight schools, hundreds of children, four musical bands and five independent artists were involved, all co-ordinated by the Community Development Manager for the Hall for Cornwall Amanda Simpson.

The crowds began to gather early and by six o'clock much of the city centre had been closed to traffic. Food stands were doing a roaring trade and market-type stalls had been set up on the cobbles. Fortunately it stayed dry, loads of listeners came along to have a chat and collect a signed photograph and everyone seemed in a festive mood. The moment the first drum beat echoed off the granite buildings, though, the atmosphere changed. Menacing and celebratory at the same time, the dozens of drums which made up bands such as Drumba and Samba Kernow made sure that everyone knew that the lanterns were about to start to make their way through the crowds.

Two separate processions began in different parts of the town, each accompanied by the bands and the huge puppet-like willow sculptures made by local artists glowed eerily overhead. A giant rat of death, a locust and a massive oriental warrior towered over the heads of the crowds supported on bamboo poles. Each of the figures reflected the millennial theme of eliminating war, pestilence and hunger and, in turn, was followed by the dozens of smaller lanterns made and carried by children from local primary schools. The processions met up and came together in the city centre with a final crescendo of music. For my money this was a real winter celebration of sound and light - not at all like the tacky commercialised idea of Christmas that was on sale in the shops all around us with their fake snow, gaudy glitter and carols-on-CD. "Goodwill to all men" may still be a far off Christmas wish but City of Lights certainly brought it that much closer.

THE MOUSEHOLE LIGHTS
December

One of the most frustrating things about Christmas - along with not being able to find the end of the roll of sticky tape when you're wrapping parcels and forgetting to defrost the turkey until Christmas morning - is the annual untangling of the fairy lights when they come out their cardboard box in the attic. Spare a thought, then, for the villagers of Mousehole in West Penwith who every year celebrate Christmas with five miles of cabling and over six thousand bulbs!

These days the Mousehole Lights are big business - some years the event's attracted European funding - and every year it manages to bring hundreds of thousands of pounds into the local economy. But as is so often the case it began in a small way. In 1963 artist Joan Gillchrist, who has a home in the village, donated a single string of lights to brighten the place up a bit and every year since then the scale of the event has grown. Letters three metres high stalk across the hillside spelling out "Merry Christmas". A whale spouts in the harbour. Champagne pops and is poured into glasses and Father Christmas and his reindeer race as silhouettes against the sky. Of course raising funds and maintaining the lights is more or less a full time job for dozens of volunteers.

A couple of years ago I went to Mousehole to meet Bob Keates and his trusty team. Known locally as the Mousehole Electric Light Bulb Company (motto: "Let There Be Lights!") with Chairman Dudley Penrose they'd begun several months earlier to unearth boxes of bulbs and drums of cable from the attics and cellars where they'd been squirrelled away. Designer Stuart Purnell had been having whispered conversations in shop doorways (each year they try to think up a new design as a surprise) and the noise of hammering and sawing had been heard coming from an old pilchard shed, which now doubles as their store, hidden in one of the village's narrow alleyways. The old wooden door of the shed swung back and I went inside.

This was a real Christmas grotto. Bright red and yellow fish boxes filled with round coloured bulbs like boiled sweets lay on the cobbles and sawdust floor. Chains of blue and green lanterns hung from the eaves and the word "WELCOME" was spelled out in an arc of letters each a metre high and studded with jewel lights. In the darkness of the furthest corners of the shed, where the daylight barely penetrated, I could make out the shapes of two or three men working away - for all the world like elves helping Father Christmas - carving and wiring, painting and glueing. Their gifts were put, not on a sleigh, but on a wooden former fish cart now painted in green and gold waiting for the day when it would be trundled down to the harbour and its cargo hung on lampposts and floated on rafts.

The Pendeen Silver Band blew for all it was worth at this year's switch on and the voices of the Mousehole Male Voice Choir and the Ladies Chapel Chorus drifted out over the sea as thousands of people thronged the streets - many of them

having come many miles to see a display that's been compared to London's Oxford Street Lights and Blackpool's Illuminations.

Each year since 1981, on one day for one hour the Christmas celebrations are stopped though and, poignantly, the lights are extinguished except for a solitary Holy Cross. It's to commemorate the Penlee lifeboat disaster which happened that year on the 19th December when the eight local crewmen of the *Solomon Browne* were lost near Lamorna in ferocious conditions. This year the weather was kind and the grey sea was calm, sparkling with the reflection of hundreds of bulbs, but of course the sheltering granite arms of the harbour reaching out into the water are there for a very good reason.

The tale is that a couple of hundred years or so ago the winter storms had been so bad that local fishermen had not been able to put to sea for weeks on end. The village was starving. The days passed until two nights before Christmas one ship's captain, Tom Bawcock, steered his boat out through the harbour mouth and, against all the odds, caught seven sorts of fish. Back ashore in Mousehole he was hailed a hero and the fish were baked into a "starry gazey pie" with the fish heads sticking out through the pastry.

Tom Bawcock's story has a timeless quality to it (this is almost the stuff of Greek legend, let me tell you) which has made it incredibly popular all over the world. It became the subject of a children's book in 1990 by illustrator Nicola Bayley and author Antonia Barber who has a home in the village and who once told me that the tale was one of the things that made her want to live there. "The Mousehole Cat" (which has Tom's cat Mowzer as the hero) went on to become an animated film which, bizarrely, I saw for the first time as an in flight movie. It seemed very strange to be so many miles away from Cornwall - not to say so many thousands of feet up in the air - being transported back home by the film's clever drawings and Sian Phillips' wonderful narration.

On the night of December 23rd there is nowhere else to be other than the Ship Inn. Here, this year like every year, star gazey pie was made and served with Leslie Nicholls dressed as Tom Bawcock himself (complete with a bowler and a huge, fake, ginger beard) taking pride of place in the bar. Locals and visitors crowd into the pub, the traditional song is sung and copious pints of beer are drunk.

Back in 1984 I was asked to appear on the children's TV programme "Saturday SuperStore" with a star gazey pie when they organised an outside broadcast from Cornwall. Unlike radio, TV work, even when it's live, is so complicated and so many people are involved that there often has to be one rehearsal after another, and after a few hours the fish heads in the pie that I was supposed to be serving, looked rather the worse for wear and were gazing rather too closely down at the pastry and not up at the stars. I'm sure that old Tom wouldn't have approved, but a packet of ballpoint pens, hurriedly bought from the local newsagent, came to the rescue. One of the production team and I quickly pulled all the fish heads out of the pie and, using the pens as skewers, impaled each of the heads and stuck them back into the crust. The director called "Action!". I smiled, the fish gazed skywards and everyone was happy although no-one could understand why I didn't eat any myself!

So, in Mousehole in December, while the shipping forecast might be warning of gales and high seas, log fires blaze in cottage hearths and cats curl up on arm chairs while the villagers look out at their own Christmas star. It might just be a few yellow bulbs roped to old ships' timbers but its message of comfort and joy is just the same.

AFTERWORD

When I set out to write about my *Year in Cornwall* I really wasn't sure what lay in store. I knew that there were a whole host of fetes and concerts and talks of one sort or another that I went to as a BBC Radio Cornwall presenter and I knew that traditional celebrations like Padstow's May Day and Crying The Neck that I went to privately would fit in somewhere too.

What I wasn't prepared for was the enormous range of events that happen in Cornwall every month of the year. Trying to keep track of them all meant that the kitchen calendar was covered in scribbles and, sadly, there were just too many to squeeze all of them into this book. There were also air days, exhibitions, agricultural shows and steam rallies. Rugby matches, ladies' luncheon clubs and lifeboat days as well as a whole host of others kept me busy too. Looking back at my diary I see that I've been to events which involved everything from going up in the air to down underground as well as on (and even under!) the sea.

However enjoyable the events themselves were it was the people who made them extra special. Wherever I went I met people who not only loved what they were doing but also the place in which they were doing it. Despite Cornwall's problems over the past few years if just some of those I spoke to have a hand in it then a year in Cornwall is going to continue to be pretty special for everyone for some time to come.